The Art of Living

WORKS BY DIETRICH VON HILDEBRAND

IN ENGLISH
Man and Woman †
The Art of Living †
Liturgy and Personality †
Transformation in Christ †
Jaws of Death: Gate of Heaven †
Trojan Horse in the City of God †
Marriage: The Mystery of Faithful Love †
In Defense of Purity
Fundamental Moral Attitudes
Ethics
The New Tower of Babel
Situation Ethics
Graven Images
What Is Philosophy?
Not as the World Gives
The Heart
The Devastated Vineyard
Celibacy and the Crisis of Faith
The Encyclical *Humanae Vitae*
Satan at Work

IN GERMAN
Die Idee der sittlichen Handlung
Sittlichkeit und ethische Werterkenntnis
Metaphysik der Gemeinschaft
Das katholische Berufsethos
Engelbert Dollfuss: Ein katholischer Staatsmann
Zeitliches im Lichte des Ewigen
Der Sinn philosophischen Fragens und Erkennens
Die Menschheit am Scheideweg
Mozart, Beethoven, Schubert
Heiligkeit und Tüchtigkeit
Das Wesen der Liebe
Die Dankbarkeit
Ästhetik I & II
Moralia

† *Available from Sophia Institute Press*

Dietrich & Alice
von Hildebrand

The Art of Living

Revised and expanded edition

SOPHIA INSTITUTE PRESS
Manchester, New Hampshire

Sophia Institute Press
Box 5284, Manchester, NH 03108
1-800-888-9344

Library of Congress Cataloging-in-Publication Data

Von Hildebrand, Dietrich, 1899-1977
    The art of living / Dietrich von Hildebrand and Alice
    von Hildebrand. — rev. and expanded ed.
       p. cm.
    ISBN 0-918477-20-4
    1. Christian life — Catholic authors. I. Von Hildebrand, Alice.
    II. Title.
    BX2350.2.V6   1993
    248.4'82—dc20   93-37484 CIP

94 95 96 97 98 99 10 9 8 7 6 5 4 3 2 1

"Congregavit nos in unum Christi amor."

To Madeleine and Lyman

Note: New Testament quotations in this book are taken from the Confraternity of Christian Doctrine edition (Paterson, N.J.: St. Anthony Guild Press, 1941). Old Testament quotations are taken from the Douay-Rheims edition. Where appropriate, quotations from Psalms are cross-referenced with the differing enumeration in the Revised Standard Version, using the following symbol: (RSV=).

Table of Contents

Foreword
By Alice von Hildebrand

"Who is the man who loves life, who desires the day in order to enjoy good things? Keep thy tongue from evil, and thy lips from deceitful words. Turn away from evil and do good, seek after peace and pursue it."[1]

Never in the history of mankind has the average man had so many material possessions and yet never has he been more restless and unhappy. All of us know people who have everything and enjoy nothing. Unhappiness pervades every aspect of their lives: their possessions have become burdens which grant immediate satisfaction but do not lead them an inch closer to happiness.

We can achieve pleasures; but no pleasure — regardless of its intensity — can satisfy the longing of the human soul. Man is made for better things.

There is something paradoxical in the fact that men yearn so deeply for happiness (which Aristotle claims to be the highest

---

[1] Psalm 33:13-15 (RSV= Ps. 34:12-14).

good) and yet so often choose paths which cannot possibly lead them to that goal. Man is often the artisan of his own doom, his own worst enemy.

Today, we rarely meet people whose faces radiate joy and peace. When they do happen to cross our paths, we wish to wrench from them the secret of their joy. What is the precious key that they have found but we do not possess?

The answer is that they have discovered the meaning of human existence, and have mastered the most important and yet the most difficult of all arts, *the art of living*. By choosing to live rightly, they have been rewarded with a peace "that the world cannot give." [2]

This small book offers you basic guidelines about how you can reach this goal. A wise and prudent guide, it will help you learn how to truly live and how, finally, to be happy.

[2] John 14:27.

Editor's Note

In the early 1930's Dietrich von Hildebrand gave a series of radio talks in Germany explaining the virtues necessary to a good and happy life. Because his talks were broadcast to a very large public, von Hildebrand wrote them in a style easily understandable by people who have no philosophical training.

His talks were so well received that they were published in 1934 under the title *Sittliche Grundhaltung* ("fundamental moral attitudes"). In 1950 Alice von Hildebrand translated *Sittliche Grundhaltung* into English and Longmans Green and Company published her translation as *Fundamental Moral Attitudes*.

Fifteen years later (in 1965), Franciscan Herald Press published an expanded edition, adding to the original book two chapters by Dietrich von Hildebrand ("Virtue Today" and "The Human Heart") and two by Alice von Hildebrand ("Communion" and "Hope"). The 1965 edition was entitled *The Art of Living*.

This 1994 Sophia Institute Press edition replaces "Virtue Today" and "The Human Heart" with the very first English translation of Dietrich von Hildebrand's posthumous booklet *"Über der*

Dankbarkeit" ("On Gratitude"). This substitution creates a more unified book, but is appropriate, as well, because Dietrich von Hildebrand sees gratitude as the crowning virtue and the key to happiness. It is therefore appropriate that the other virtues discussed in this expanded edition of *The Art of Living* be completed by gratitude as their crowning chapter.

The Art of Living

Reverence

Moral values are the highest among all natural values. Goodness, purity, truthfulness, and humility rank higher than genius, brilliance, and exuberant vitality, higher than the beauty of nature or of art, and higher than the stability and power of a state.

Moral values are the highest natural values

That which is realized and shines forth in an act of genuine forgiveness, in a noble and generous renunciation, in a burning and selfless love, is more significant and more noble, more important and more eternal than all cultural values. Positive moral values are the focus of the world; negative moral values are the greatest evil, worse than suffering, sickness, death, or the disintegration of a flourishing culture.

This fact was recognized by great thinkers such as Socrates or Plato, who continually repeated that it is better to suffer injustice than to commit it. This preeminence of the moral sphere is, above all, a basic proposition of the Christian ethos.

Only persons can bear moral values

Moral values are always personal values. They can only inhere in and be realized by man. A material thing, like a stone or a house, cannot be morally good or bad, just as moral goodness is not possible to a tree or a dog. Similarly, works of the human mind (for example, discoveries, scientific books, and works of art), cannot properly be said to be the bearers of moral values; they cannot be faithful, humble, and loving. They can, at the most, indirectly reflect these values as bearing the imprint of the human mind. Man alone (as a free being, responsible for his actions and his attitudes, for his will and striving, his love and his hatred, his joy and his sorrow, and his superactual basic attitude) can be morally good or bad. For far above his cultural accomplishments rises the importance of man's own being: a personality radiating moral values, a man who is humble, pure, truthful, honest, and loving.

Moral goodness comes from the right response to values

But how can man participate in these moral values? Are they given to him by nature like the beauty of his face, his intelligence, or a lively temperament? No, they can only grow out of conscious, free attitudes; man himself must essentially cooperate for their realization. They can only develop through his conscious, free abandonment of himself to genuine values. Man will be rich in moral values in proportion to his capacity to grasp values, insofar as he sees the fullness of the world of values with a clear and fresh vision, and insofar as his abandonment to this world is pure and unconditional.

As long as a man blindly disregards the moral values of other persons, as long as he does not distinguish the positive value which inheres in truth and the negative value which is proper to error, as long as he does not understand the positive value which inheres in the life of man and the negative value attached to an injustice, he will be incapable of moral goodness. As long as he is only interested in the question of whether something is subjectively satisfying or not, whether it is agreeable to him or not, he cannot be morally good.

The soul of every morally good attitude is abandonment to that which is objectively important, is interest in a thing because it has value. Two men are, for example, witnesses of an injustice which is being inflicted upon a third person. The one who in every situation asks only whether something is agreeable to himself will not be concerned about the injustice because he calculates that no personal damage to himself can result from the other's injury. The second man, on the contrary, is willing to take suffering upon himself rather than remain disinterested in the injustice which is about to be done to the third person. For the second man, the preponderant question is not whether something is agreeable to him or not, but whether it is *important in itself*. The second man behaves morally well, the first one morally badly because he indifferently bypasses the question of value.

Whether a person chooses or rejects an agreeable thing which is indifferent from the point of view of value, depends upon his own pleasure. Whether he does or does not eat an excellent meal is up to himself. But positive value calls for an affirmation and negative value for a refusal on our part.

Confronted with these, the way in which we should behave is not left to our arbitrary pleasure. Instead it should be the subject of preoccupation and the right response should be given, for interest in values and adequate responses to them are due to values. Whether one does or does not help another person who is in need does not depend upon one's arbitrary pleasure; he is guilty who ignores this objective value.

Only he who understands that there exist things important in themselves, that there are things which are beautiful and good in themselves, only the man who grasps the sublime demand of values, their call, and the duty to turn toward them and to let oneself be formed by their law, is capable of personally realizing moral values. Only the man who can see beyond his subjective horizon and who, free from pride and concupiscence, does not always ask "what is satisfying for me?" but who, leaving behind him all narrowness, abandons himself to that which is important in itself — the beautiful, the good — and subordinates himself to it, only he can become the bearer of moral values.

Only the reverent give the proper response to values

The capacity to grasp values, to affirm them, and to respond to them is the foundation for realizing the moral values of man.

Now these marks can be found only in the man who possesses reverence. Reverence is the attitude which can be designated as the mother of all moral life, for in it man first takes a position toward the world which opens his spiritual eyes and enables him to grasp values. Consequently, in these chapters which deal with moral attitudes (that is to say, attitudes which give a basis to the whole of moral life and are presupposed for this life), we must first of all speak of this virtue.

The irreverent and impertinent man is incapable of any aban-donment or subordination of self. He is the slave of his pride, of that cramping egoism which makes him a prisoner of himself, blind to values, and leads him to ask repeatedly "will my prestige be increased, will my own glory be augmented?" Or he is a slave of concupiscence, one for whom everything in the world becomes only an occasion to serve his lust. The irreverent man can never remain inwardly silent. He never gives situations, things, and persons a chance to unfold themselves in their proper character and value. He approaches everything in such an importunate and tactless way that he observes only himself, listens only to himself, and ignores the rest of being. He does not preserve a reverent distance from the world.

Irreverence may be rooted in pride

Irreverence can be divided into two types according to whether it is rooted in pride or in concupiscence. The first type is that of the man whose irreverence is a fruit of his pride, that of the impertinent person. He is the type of man who approaches everything with a presumptuous, sham superiority, and never makes any effort to understand a thing *from within*. He is the "know-it-all" schoolmaster type who believes that he penetrates everything at first sight and knows all things right from the start. He is the man for whom nothing could be greater than himself, who never sees beyond his own horizon, from whom the world of being hides no secret. He is the man Shakespeare has in mind in *Hamlet*: "There are more things in heaven and earth, Horatio, than are dreamt of in your philosophy."

He is the man possessed of a blighting incomprehension, without yearnings, like Famulus in Goethe's *Faust* who is completely filled by 'how wondrously far he has gone.' This man suspects nothing of the breadth and depth of the world, of the mysterious depths and the immeasurable fullness of values which are bespoken by every ray of the sun and every plant, and which are revealed in the innocent laughter of a child, as well as in the repentant tears of a sinner. The world is flattened before his impertinent and stupid gaze; it becomes limited to one dimension, shallow and mute. It is evident that such a man is blind to values. He passes through the world with a blighting incomprehension.

Irreverence may be rooted in concupiscence

The other type of man who lacks reverence — the blunt, concupiscent man — is equally blind to values. He limits his interest to one thing only: whether something is agreeable to him or not, whether it offers him satisfaction, whether it can be of any use to him.

He sees in all things only that dimension which is related to his accidental, immediate interest. Every being is, for him, but a means to his own selfish aim. He drags himself about eternally in the circle of his narrowness and never actually succeeds in emerging from himself. Consequently, he also does not know the true and deep happiness which can only flow from abandonment to true values, from contact with that which is in itself good and beautiful.

He does not approach being as does the first type in an impertinent way, but he is equally closed up within himself and does not preserve that distance toward being required by reverence. He overlooks all things and seeks only that which is momentarily useful and expedient to him.

Similarly, he can never be inwardly silent, or open his spiritual self to the influence of being. He can never allow himself to receive the joy that values give. He is also, as it were, in a perpetual ego spasm. His look falls on all things flatly, from the outside, without comprehension for the true meaning and value of an object.

He also is shortsighted, and comes too close to all things, so that he does not give them a chance to reveal their true essence. He fails to leave to any being the "space" which it needs to unfold itself fully and in its proper mode. This man also is blind to values, and to him again the world refuses to reveal its breadth, depth, and height.

The reverent man sees reality as it is

The man possessing reverence approaches the world in a completely different way. He is free from this ego spasm, from pride and concupiscence. He does not fill the world with his own ego, but leaves to being the space which it needs in order to unfold itself. He understands the dignity and nobility of being as such, the value which it already possesses in its opposition to mere nothingness. Thus there is a value inherent in every stone, in a drop of water, in a blade of grass, precisely as being, as an entity which possesses its own being, which is such and not otherwise. In contradistinction to a fantasy or a sheer semblance, being is something independent of the person considering it and withdrawn from that person's arbitrary will. Hence each of these things has the general value of existence.

The reverent man does not see things as instruments

Because of this autonomy, being is never a *mere* means for the reverent man and his accidental egoistic aims. Being is never merely something which he can use. Rather, he takes it seriously in itself; he leaves it the necessary space for its proper unfolding. Confronted with being, the reverent man remains silent in order to give it an opportunity to speak.

The man who possesses reverence knows that the world of being is greater than he is, that he is not the Lord who can do with things as He likes, and that he must learn from being, not the other way around.

This responsive attitude to the value of being is pervaded by the disposition to recognize something superior to one's arbitrary pleasure and will, and to be ready to subordinate and abandon oneself to it. It enables the spiritual eye to see the deeper nature of every being. It leaves to being the possibility of unveiling its essence and makes a man capable of grasping values.

To whom will the sublime beauty of a sunset or the Ninth Symphony of Beethoven reveal itself, but to him who approaches it reverently and unlocks his heart to it?

To whom will the mystery which lies in life and which manifests itself in every plant reveal itself in its full splendor, but to the person who contemplates it reverently? But he who sees in it only a means of subsistence or of earning money (that is, as something which can be used or employed) will not discover the meaning, structure, and significance of the world in its beauty and hidden dignity.

Reverence is presupposed for knowledge of values

Reverence is the indispensable presupposition for all deep knowledge — above all, for the capacity to grasp values. All capacity to be made happy and uplifted by values, all sanctioned abandonment to values, all submission to their majesty, presupposes reverence.

In reverence the person takes into account the sublimity of the world of values; in it he finds that upward look toward that world, that respect for the objective and valid demands immanent to the values which, independently of the arbitrary will and wishes of men, call for an adequate response.

Reverence is the presupposition for every response to value, every abandonment to something important, and is at the same time an essential element of such response to value. Each time one gives oneself to the good and beautiful, each time one conforms to the inner law of value, the basic attitude of reverence is implied. This can be verified by examining moral attitudes on the different levels of life.

Reverence is an essential element of love

The fundamental attitude of reverence is the basis for all moral conduct toward our fellowmen and toward ourselves. Only to the man possessing reverence is revealed the full grandeur and depth of the values which inhere in every man as a spiritual person. The spiritual person as a conscious, free being, as a being who, alone among all the entities known to us, is capable of knowing and grasping the rest of being and of taking a meaningful position toward it, can only be comprehended by a reverent mind. A being who is able and destined to realize in himself a rich world of values, to become a vessel of goodness, purity, and humility — this is a person.

How could one really love another person, how could he make sacrifices for him, if he sensed nothing of the preciousness and plenitude which is potentially enclosed in man's soul, if he had no reverence for this being?

The basic attitude of reverence is the presupposition for every true love — and, above all, for love of neighbor — because reverence alone opens our eyes to the value of men as spiritual persons, and because, without this awareness, no love is possible.

Reverence for the beloved is also an essential element of every love. To give attention to the specific meaning and value of his individuality, to display consideration toward him instead of forcing our wishes on him, is part reverence.

It is from reverence that there flows the willingness of a lover to grant the beloved the spiritual "space" needed to express freely his own individuality. All these elements of every true love flow from reverence.

What would mother love be without reverence for the growing being, for all the possibilities of values which yet lie dormant, for the preciousness of the child's soul?

Justice presupposes reverence

A similar reverence is evident in justice toward others, in consideration for the rights of another, for the liberty of another's decision, in limiting one's own lust for power, and in all understanding of another's rights. Reverence for our neighbors is the basis for all true community life, for the right approach to marriage, the family, the nation, the state, humanity, for respect of legitimate authority, for the fulfillment of moral duties toward the community as a whole and toward the individual members of it. The irreverent man splits and disintegrates community.

Purity presupposes reverence

But reverence is also the soul of the correct attitude in other domains, such as purity. Reverence for the mystery of the marital union, for the depth, tenderness, and the decisive and lasting validity of this most intimate abandonment of self, is the presupposition for purity. First of all, reverence assures an understanding of this sphere; it shows us how horrible is every illicit approach to this mysterious domain, since such an illicit approach desecrates us and involves a serious debasement of our dignity and that of others. Reverence for the wonder of the coming into being of a new life out of the closest union of love of two people is the basis for the horror of every artificial and irreverent act destroying this mysterious bond which exists between love and the coming into being of new men.

Religion presupposes reverence

Wherever we look, we see reverence to be the basis and at the same time an essential element of moral life and moral values.

Without a fundamental attitude of reverence, no true love, no justice, no kindliness, no self-development, no purity, no truthfulness are possible. Above all, without reverence, the dimension of depth is completely excluded. The irreverent person is himself flat and shallow, for he fails to understand the depth of being, since for him there is no world beyond and above that which is visibly palpable. Only to the man possessing reverence does the world of religion open itself; only to him will the world as a whole reveal its meaning and value. So reverence as a basic moral attitude stands at the beginning of all religion. It is the basis for the right attitude of men toward themselves, their neighbors, to every level of being, and above all to God.

Faithfulness

Among the attitudes of man which are basic for his whole moral life, faithfulness is ranked next to reverence. One can speak of faithfulness in a narrow sense and in a large one. We have the narrow sense in mind when we speak of fidelity toward men (such as fidelity to a friend, marital fidelity, fidelity to one's country or to oneself).

Faithfulness gives life continuity

This type of fidelity throws into relief the other type. I refer here to the continuity which first gives to a man's life its inner consistency, its inner unity. The building up of one's personality is only possible if one holds firmly to those truths and values which one has already discovered.

The course of a man's life contains a continual rhythmical replacement of one impression, one act, one decision by another and different impression, act, or decision. We are unable to ponder one thought for a long time and to keep our attention on one point for very long. Just as in the biological realm, hunger and satiety, fatigue and renewed strength succeed one another, so a certain rhythmical change is proper to the course of our spiritual life. Just as the various impressions which affect us give place to one another, and the stream of events offers to our mind a great variety of objects, so our attention cannot long remain focused on any one object with the same intensity. A movement from one subject to another is therefore proper to our thought, as well as to our feeling and will. Even in the case of a very blissful experience, such as the long-desired meeting with a beloved person, we are unable to dwell permanently in this joyous experience. The rhythm of our inner life forces us to leave the full presence of a great joy and to turn our attention in another direction and to register different experiences.

Deep continuity is the foundation of personality

But — and this must be stressed — the same man has different levels of depth. The psychic life of man is not restricted to the level on which this continual change unfolds itself; it is not restricted to the level of our express attention, of our present consciousness. While we proceed to another impression and give our attention to another mental object, the preceding impression or object does not vanish, but will, according to its significance, be retained and will continue to live on a deeper level. Memory is an expression of this capacity of the soul for superactual life, and this continuity is seen in our capacity to remember, to connect past and present.

Above all, we see this continuity in the superactual survival of our attitudes toward the world, toward fundamental truths and values, which remain unchanged even though our present attention is turned in a completely different direction. Thus, for example, joy caused by some happy event continues to "live" in the depth of our souls and colors everything we do, all our tasks of the moment, and our approach to all those things with which we are expressly concerned. So also our love for a beloved person remains living in the depth of our souls, even though we are occupied by work, and this love constitutes a sort of background against which different events run their course. Without this capacity for continuity, man would have no inner unity; he would be but a bundle of interwoven impressions and experiences. If one impression merely took the place of the preceding one, if the past should indiscriminately vanish, the inner life of man would be senseless and shallow; any building up, any development would be impossible. Above all, there would be no personality.

Men have different degrees of inner continuity

Even though this capacity of retaining impressions and attitudes in a superactual way, without which the individual life of a spiritual person is impossible, is a capacity common to every man, the degree to which a given individual possesses this inner continuous coherence is very different in each case. We say of many men that they live in the moment only; the present instant has such power over them that the past, even though its content be deeper and more important, vanishes before the insistent clamor of the present.

Men differ very much from each other in this regard. Some of them live exclusively on the exterior level of their present consciousness, so that one experience follows another without any relation to the one preceding. We could call such men "butterflies." Others, on the contrary, also live in the deeper level of their being. In them nothing important is sacrificed because it is no longer present, but it becomes the unalterable possession of the man, according to its degree of importance, and new meaningful experiences organically unite themselves with it. The last type alone can be said to have *personality*. Only in this type of man can an inner spiritual plenitude be constituted.

Inconstant men are prisoners of immediate impressions

How many people there are who are never lastingly influenced by great works of art, by delight in beautiful landscapes, or by contact with great personalities. The momentary impression may be strong but it strikes no deep root in them; it is not firmly held in their superactual life but disappears as soon as another impression makes its appearance. These men are like a sieve through which everything runs. Although they can be good, kindly, and honest, they cleave to a childish, unconscious position; they have no depth. They elude one's grasp; they are incapable of having deep relationships with other people because they are capable of no permanent relationship with anything. These men do not know responsibility because they know no lasting bond, because with them one day does not reach into the next one. Even though their impressions are strong, these impressions do not penetrate down to the deepest level in which we find attitudes which are over and above the changes of the moment. These people honestly promise something one moment and in the next it has completely disappeared from their memory. They make resolutions under a strong impression, but the next impression blows them away. They are so impressionable that they are always held at the superficial level of their present consciousness. For these people, weight and value are not the preponderant factors determining their interest in things, but only the liveliness of the impression created by the actual presence of these things. What makes an impression upon them is the general advantage of *liveliness* which present impressions or situations have over those of the past.

Superficial men are inconstant

There are two types of inconstant men. In the one, nothing ever truly penetrates to their deeper center. This deeper center, so to speak, remains void in them; they know only the strata of present consciousness. These men are at the same time superficial, deprived of profound life and of any sort of inner *firmness*. They are like quicksand which yields without any resistance. If you seek in such men a permanent center upon which you can depend and rely, then you really snatch at the void.

Of course, in a healthy man this is not absolutely and completely the case; a man who, in a literal sense, would be completely of this character would be a psychopath. But we often meet people whose lives, at least to a certain extent, unfold themselves in such a manner, although we could not therefore call them psychotic.

Deeper men can also be inconstant

In the second type, we have to deal with men who actually do have deep impressions, in whose deeper strata much really does take root. Their deeper consciousness is therefore not void; they have created in themselves a firm, lasting center. But they are so imprisoned in the present moment that that which lies in their deeper strata is unable to carry its true weight; it cannot hold its ground against the power of the momentary impression. Only when the present, lively impression fades away can the content of the deeper strata again come to light. Such men could, for example, very well nourish a deep, lasting love for another person, but a momentary situation, if it happens to be powerful, vivid, and appealing, would capture them to such an extent that the beloved one would be almost forgotten. Then they say and do things which contradict the genuine and living love hidden in the depths of their souls. Such people are continually in danger of becoming traitors to themselves or to others. For such persons, the individual who is present, merely because he is present, has always the advantage over the absent. This is the case even when the absent person is, on the whole, dearer to them and in the long run plays a more important role. Suppose they have, for example, received a deep impression from a work of art; a lasting relation to this work of art has constituted itself in the depths of their souls. Nevertheless, new powerful impressions take hold of them to such an extent that the prior impression is not firmly held in the new situation, and as a result one sees no trace of the first impression as long as the new one lasts. Later, when the immersing effect of the new situation has worn off, the old one, in itself deeper, reenters into possession of its rightful place and authority.

Persevering men are faithful to perennial values

In contradistinction to these two types, the persevering man holds on to everything which has revealed itself to him as a genuine value. The advantage of liveliness, which the present possesses over the past, has no power over his life when compared to the inner weight of deep truths which he has once recognized and of values which he has once grasped. The importance of the role played by a given thing in his present consciousness is exclusively determined by the height of its value, and in no way by its mere presence.

Fidelity protects us from the tyranny of fashion

Such men are, consequently, protected from the tyranny of fashion. A thing never makes a deep impression upon them merely because it is modern, because it is momentarily "in the air," but only because it has a value, because it is beautiful, good, and true. As a matter of fact, these persons consider that which is more important and has a higher value as itself the more "up to date." Objects endowed with values never grow old for them, even if the concrete existence of these objects ceased long ago. The lives of these men are meaningfully integrated and in their course reflect the objective gradation of values. While the inconstant man is a prey to accidental impressions and situations, the constant man dominates his own impressions. Such men alone understand the sublime preeminence of values over any mere dimension of time, the unchanging and unfading character of values and truth. They understand that an important truth is not less interesting and less worthy of concern because we have known it for a long time. They understand, above all, that the obligation to respond to a good possessing a value is not limited to the moment in which it is grasped.

Only the man who is constant really grasps the demands of the world of values; only he is capable of the response to value which is due to objective values. A proper response to values is lasting, and is independent of the charm of novelty and of the attractive force represented by the mere presence of a thing. He alone for whom values never lose their efficacy and charm once they have been revealed to him, and who never lets a truth which he has grasped drop into oblivion, will really do justice to the proper character of the world of truth and values. He alone is capable of remaining faithful to objects possessing value.

Fidelity is essential to moral maturity

This constancy or fidelity in the true sense of the word is, as we see, a fundamental moral attitude of man. It is a necessary consequence of all true understanding of values, and it is a component element of every true response to values and consequently of the whole moral life.

Only the constant response to values, the response which clings to a thing possessing a value (whether that thing is actually present or not), is a developed, morally mature, and fully conscious response to value. Only a man who responds in this way is truly morally awakened; he alone is reliable. He alone feels himself to be responsible for that which he has done in other situations; he alone is capable of true contrition for previous misdeeds. In him alone all true obligations will dominate every situation of his life. He alone will stand firm in trials. For the light of values will shine for him even in the humdrum situations of workaday life — yes, even at the moments of temptation.

This is so because this man lives from the depth and masters every moment from the depth. The more faithful, the more constant a man is, the richer and more substantial he will be, the more capable of becoming a vessel of moral values, a being in whom purity, justice, humility, love, and goodness will dwell lastingly and from whom those values will radiate to the world about him.

Fidelity is essential to spiritual growth

Were we to examine the different levels of life, we would find over and over again the basic significance of faithfulness in this larger sense. The basic attitude of constancy is a general presupposition for all spiritual growth of the person, and above all for every moral development and every moral progress. How can a man grow spiritually who does not firmly adhere to all the values which have been revealed to him, and for whom these values do not become a lasting possession? How could one who is dominated by short-lived momentary impressions ever succeed in a gradual development of his own moral structure?

Inconstancy stunts moral development

When we have to deal with the radically inconstant man we first mentioned in this chapter, we see that nothing at all reaches down into such a person's deeper strata. Such men are inwardly dead; their personality lacks a lasting center. In men of the second type, there is lacking the possibility of a real formation of the course of life; for the values they once grasped — and which should be a permanent possession of their souls — have disappeared from their lives. They cannot therefore mold new impressions by such values. What is the use of the best education if this constancy is missing? What is the use of the most pressing exhortations, of the most vivid revelation of values, if values once grasped remain either without any permanent roots or if they slumber in our souls? As surprising as it may sound, inconstant people never change themselves. They retain the faults and features which they have inherited from their nature, but they acquire no moral values. Even though they really do for a moment recognize their faults and form the best resolutions, their inconstancy prevents any lasting moral improvement. Even when their will is good, education will have no lasting effect upon them. This is not because they close themselves up (like the man who is victim of a cramping pride and to whom therefore the influence of values cannot penetrate) but because they give too much weight to every fleeting impression and are thus unable to retain what they have acquired.

Inconstancy interferes with learning

All self-education presupposes this attitude of constancy. The constant man alone will be able to assimilate contradictory impressions so as to draw that which is good out of each. He will learn from every situation of life and will grow in every situation, for in him the measure of genuine values remains alive. The inconstant man, on the other hand, yields now to one, now to another impression, and becomes so entirely a prey of each that in the depth of his soul everything passes on more or less without leaving a trace. This gradually withers his comprehension of values and his susceptibility to their influence. The constant man alone will prefer what is more important to what is less so, what is more valuable to the less, while the inconstant person will at best respond indiscriminately to all values, recognizing no hierarchy in them. In fact, nothing is more important for moral growth, for the very moral life of a person, than consideration for the objective hierarchy of values and the capacity to give priority to that which is objectively higher.

Morality and religion presuppose constancy

The fundamental attitude of fidelity is also the presupposition for reliability in every moral trial. How can he who lives only in the present moment, in whom the past, present and future do not form significant unity, keep a promise or stand the test in a battle of ideas? How can one rely upon such an inconstant person? The faithful man alone can inspire that confidence which forms the basis of any community. He alone possesses the high moral value of stability, reliability, and trustworthiness.

But constancy is also a condition for any confidence on the part of the person himself and above all for heroic faith. The unstable man is not only undeserving of confidence, but he himself will be incapable of a firm, unshakeable confidence either in other men, in truth, or in God Himself.

Such a man lacks the strength to nourish his soul upon a value once discovered. Therefore when night and obscurity surround him, or when other strong impressions assail him, he loses faith. It is no accident that in Latin the word *fides* means both "fidelity" and "faith." For constancy is an essential constituent of all capacity to believe, and consequently, of all religion.

Faithfulness is at the heart of every love

The eminent importance of faithfulness will stand out in a special way against the background of human relationships. (Here *faithfulness* is taken in its narrow sense, i.e., "fidelity.") For what is love without fidelity? In the ultimate analysis, it is nothing but a lie. For the deepest meaning of every love — the inner "word" uttered in love — is the interior orientation toward and giving of oneself to the beloved, a giving which knows no time limit. No fluctuation in the course of life can shatter it. If it is true love, only a deep change in the beloved person can affect our love if it is true love.

A man who would say "I love you now, but how long it will last, I cannot tell" does not truly love; he does not even suspect the very nature of love. Faithfulness is so essentially one with love, that everyone, at least as long as he loves, must consider his devotion an undying devotion. This holds good for every love, for parental and filial love, for friendship, and for spousal love. The deeper a love, the more it is pervaded by fidelity.

It is precisely in this faithfulness that we find the specific moral splendor, the chaste beauty of love. The especially touching element of love, as expressed so uniquely in Beethoven's *Fidelio*, is essentially tied up with fidelity. The unalterable fidelity of a mother's love, the victorious faithfulness of a friend, possess a specific moral beauty which touches the man whose heart is opened to values. Faithfulness is at the heart of every true and deep love. It is immanent to its very nature.

On the other hand, what is more base or more repulsive than outspoken unfaithfulness, that radical opposition to fidelity, which is far worse than mere inconstancy. What a heinous moral stain marks the traitor who by infidelity pierces the very heart which has confidently opened itself to him and offers itself unprotected to him. He who is unfaithful in his basic attitudes is a Judas to the world of values.

Fidelity is a free response to the world of values

There are people to whom fidelity appears in the light of a mere bourgeois virtue, a mere correctness, a technical loyalty. In the opinion of such people the man who is great, highly gifted, and freed from petty conventions has no concern with it. This is a senseless misunderstanding of the true nature of fidelity. It is true that too strong an emphasis on one's own fidelity may create a painful impression. It is true that it is possible to give a certain harmless, good-natured, and cheap imitation of fidelity. The fact remains that true faithfulness is an indispensable element of all moral greatness, of all depth and strength of personality.

Fidelity is opposed to mere bourgeois loyalty or to a pure clinging to habit. It would be an error to believe that fidelity is the mere result of a lazy temperament, and inconstancy the result of a spontaneous and vivacious one. No, this virtue is a free, meaningful response to the world of truth and of values, to the unchangeable and intrinsic importance of that world and to its real demands. Without this basic attitude of fidelity, no culture, no progress in knowledge, no community, above all no moral personality, no moral growth, no substantial, inwardly unified spiritual life, no true love are possible. This basic significance of fidelity, in the larger sense, must penetrate to the heart of every relationship if it is not to be judged as a failure.

3

Responsibility

When we call someone a *morally conscious* man, and another person a *morally unconscious* one, we have in mind a difference which is decisive from the ethical point of view.

The morally unconscious man is governed by impulse

The unconscious man drifts through life. Of course, he grasps certain values and responds to them, but this process goes on in a manner that is deprived of an ultimate *wakefulness* and of an explicit character. His grasp of values remains more or less accidental. Above all, his life, on the whole, is not consciously and expressly lived under the awful sword of good and evil. Even when, at a given moment, he rejects something bad and affirms something good, at heart this attitude is an affirmation of his own temperament rather than a really enlightened cooperation with and conformity to the implacable demands of values.

The unconscious man behaves according to the impulses of his nature; he has not yet discovered within himself the capacity to direct himself freely toward the objective demands of the world of values independently of what is or is not congenial to his nature. He is unaware of this capacity freely to approve or disavow impulses arising from his own nature according to whether they are or are not in conformity with the world of values.

Moral excellence eludes the morally unconscious man

Unconscious men are not awakened to the specifically moral prerogative of the spiritual person either to approve or to disavow freely; they make no use of it.

Consequently, they ignore the necessity for conscious effort to develop and improve their moral stature. In their lives we find no moral self-education. This moral sluggishness is an obstacle to the formation of a moral personality. Moral consciousness and moral wakefulness are indispensable presuppositions for a real grasp of values, for true responses to values and consequently for the possession of moral values. The morally unconscious man can be good, faithful, just, and a friend of truth, but only in the sense that he is a pale reflection of these virtues. His goodness, fidelity, justice, and truthfulness lack the specific beauty of moral excellence, a full and free turning to values, a submission to their sovereign majesty, and a real subordination to their eternal laws. The accidental character of such a man's virtues and the incomplete character of his responses deprive these virtues of their true moral core. They are moral virtues whose soul is deprived of its ultimate, free, meaningful life.

The morally conscious man is mindful of responsibilities

Reverence and that true fidelity which we call *constancy* are closely related to this moral wakefulness. Moreover, they can only fully unfold themselves in a morally conscious man. This moral wakefulness is also the soul of the fundamental moral attitude which we have called *awareness of responsibility.*

Only the man with this consciousness of responsibility can justly appreciate the impact of the demands of the world of values. He grasps not only the splendor, the inner beauty, and majesty of the world of values, but also the sovereignty over us which this world objectively possesses. He understands the implacable earnestness of their demands; he experiences their personal call on us. He perceives the commands and the prohibitions which issue from values.

He possesses that wakefulness toward the world of values which places his life under its sword of justice, which makes him at every moment aware of his own position and duties in the cosmos, and which makes him realize clearly that he is not his own master. He knows that he cannot act freely according to his arbitrary pleasure, that he is not his own judge, but that he must render an account to Someone who is higher than he is.

Corruption is the worst form of moral irresponsibility

The very opposite of the man who is conscious of his responses is the heedless and thoughtless man. The most radical type in this category is represented by the man who does not in the least concern himself with the world of values, but only with what is subjectively satisfying to him.

He is the coarse man, subject to his own desires, who blindly bypasses all values and for whom the whole world offers only an occasion to secure more pleasure. This is the same type of man we have designated earlier as one who lacks reverence. He lives in darkness, almost as an animal, and casts the world of values completely aside. He is not concerned with either good or evil, and takes no notice of the importance of the demands of the world of values or of the sword of justice which hangs over his head. Although he may pursue his quest of pleasure and enjoyment with remarkable cleverness and care, he is possessed by an ultimate, terrible thoughtlessness. It is obvious that this man, who is never touched by values, who knows no abandonment to them, is completely irresponsible.

Moral unconsciousness is a second form of irresponsibility

Completely different from this totally corrupted type, in whom no moral value can flower at all, is the morally unconscious man of whom we have spoken above. The latter can, to a certain extent, grasp values, be affected by them, and sometimes even conform to them, but he cannot have a full understanding of them since he is deprived of a conscious and explicit awareness.

He is also filled with a deep thoughtlessness, with a lack of realization of the ultimate importance of the world of values and its demands. He can be good-natured, amiable, generous, ready to help, but all this without an ultimate attainment of moral excellence.

This man also does not possess a consciousness of responsibility. In the different situations of life he does not seek a really clear and unequivocal decision on the question of value; to say "yes" or "no," it suffices for him to have an approximate impression of what is good or evil, what is beautiful or ugly.

This is understandable; for he does not consider the specific, objective nature of the value and its demand, but only whether a given attitude suits him or not, whether or not it is in inner conformity to his temperament. Consequently, his responses will be thoughtless, deprived of an unequivocal clarity of vision with regard to the values at stake in any concrete situation.

Superficiality leaves irresponsible some who seek goodness

Finally, there exists a type of thoughtless man who makes a conscious moral effort, but who, on account of a certain superficiality and frivolity in his nature, does not consider it necessary in making his decisions to have a clear and precise notion of the value in question. He does not exert himself to work out a clear idea of a question of value in a given case. He will make decisions in serious cases on the pure appearance of good or evil. What public opinion says, what is advised by an acquaintance, what appears to him through convention as correct suffices for him to take a position in a given case. He fails to understand that, before making a decision, the importance of the question of whether or not an adequate response has been given to values imperatively obliges us to reach a real and clear understanding regarding the demands of those values. The thoughtlessness of such men lies in the fact that they do not take the question of value seriously enough; in spite of their good will, they reach an affirmative or negative decision without having truly hearkened to the voice of values, without having taken the trouble really to examine what is due to values.

Through this lack of a sense of responsibility, the life of such a man actually becomes a sort of game played out on the surface. So long as this attitude is dominant, the man in question remains immature and childish. This attitude is also proper to the typically inconstant man, of whom we have spoken in a previous chapter, who lives only in the present moment and who cannot retain the acquisitions of his deeper experiences because of the influence of those which are present. The man lacking in a sense of responsibility also responds too quickly, without taking the trouble to test new experiences against the background of truths that he has already discovered.

The Art of Living

Irresponsibility in thought or deed is morally negative

The morally negative attitude of this lack of a sense of responsibility is particularly striking when we are dealing not only with an interior attitude, but with an exterior transient action. Obviously, every "yes" or "no" which is uttered in response to values is a part of reality, and therefore carries the whole decisive import of reality as opposed to the mere possibilities which may present themselves to our imagination.

Here again, an abyss yawns between a tendency arising in us and the inner "yes" or "no" of a fully conscious response. In every purely inner decision that we reach, in every enthusiasm or indignation freely sanctioned by us, there lies something which we cannot undo.

But an action which intervenes in the exterior world is still more irrevocable if the status *ante quo* cannot be restored. For in the case of inward attitudes, by means of an inner revocation of the past through genuine contrition, we can at least erase an essential element of what has really taken place. But he who has neglected a once-given opportunity in the sphere of external action cannot undo what he has done; he who has failed to save another man whose life is in danger cannot resuscitate him.

Irresponsibility is a form of disrespect for reality

In lack of responsibility, in thoughtlessness, there is also evident a lack of respect for reality, for the import of something which has once been brought into existence. There is as well a blighting lack of comprehension of the irrevocable character and the consequences of any evil deed. The German poet Schiller expresses this truth when he writes: "This is the curse of every evil deed / That, propagating still, it brings forth evil."

Responsibility

The thoughtless man is frightened when he realizes what he has done. His guilty deed is not the result of bad intention, but of a general and blighting lack of comprehension of the seriousness and importance of reality.

Lack of understanding of the seriousness of the demands of values, failure to respond to this aspect of the world of values, induces in him a misunderstanding of the import of reality. It is quite understandable that from a frivolous attitude toward reality there will issue decisions formed without sufficient understanding of the demands that emanate from values.

Moreover, we find such a man disinterested in the consequences of an action; his attitude is to consider only the present moment. Of course, certain consequences are not always to be foreseen, and certain demands of values are such that they, so to speak, themselves assume the responsibility of possible consequences. But in the majority of cases, we should, before making a decision, examine whether the consequences of our action, as far as they can be foreseen and still more if they are inevitable, are in themselves good or bad. Otherwise, a true interest in values would be lacking.

The responsible man takes reality seriously

The man who is aware of his responsibility, on the other hand, understands the full seriousness of the world of values and its demands, and takes these demands into account. He grasps the entire seriousness and irrevocable character of reality inherent in every decision. Insofar as it is at all possible in a given situation, he makes a decision and takes his position only when the question of value is unequivocally clear to him. His life bears the seal of wakefulness, of earnestness instead of frivolity, of manliness instead of childishness.

The Art of Living

Responsibility demands carefulness, not slowness

This does not mean that the man aware of his responsibilities must be an ultracautious person, who endlessly hesitates and endlessly deliberates before taking a stand or making a decision. In a given situation he can just as well make a choice without further deliberation, if the value at stake reveals itself at first sight in unmistakable clarity. The question of whether a man is aware of his responsibility does not depend upon whether the basis of his decision is an immediate intuition of the value or whether it is reached by deliberation. What matters exclusively is whether the value is or is not unequivocally clear to him.

What decides the specific nature of the consciously awakened man is not the difference between an ultracautious, hesitating, and slow temperament as opposed to an energetic and prompt one. No, an awakened man will act either cautiously or promptly according to whether, at first sight, he is or is not unequivocally clear concerning the value at stake. It is not his temperament, but the degree to which the values or negative values and their demands are objectively lucid to him which will lead him in one case to take an immediate and apparently impulsive position, while in another to examine the situation with concern and deliberation. Thanks to his wakefulness and reverence for the world of values and the importance of reality, he understands that before making a decision he is called upon to obtain the greatest possible evidence concerning the values at stake.

The responsible man relies upon good advisors

The man who is truly and consciously aware of his responsibility is, however, far from placing stubborn reliance upon his own insight. He has nothing in common with the so-called proud and self-assured man, who believes that he owes it to himself to base all decisions exclusively upon his own insight.

The man who is truly and consciously aware of his responsibility has nothing of this cramping egotism and this moral pride; he is, on the contrary, exclusively concerned with fulfilling the objective demands of the world of values. Such a man is also aware of the limits of his own ability and capacity to grasp values. Accordingly, he allows himself to be guided by the clear insight of someone he knows to be morally superior and to have a deeper grasp of values, rather than preferring to follow a vague impression which his own insight into a certain situation gives him.

First of all, he will be guided by the commandments of a true authority. But he himself must first be convinced beyond doubt of the superiority of his adviser in the understanding of morally relevant values, and he must clearly understand the legitimate nature of that adviser's authority. He will not allow pure suggestion to have any influence upon his decisions. He will not let himself be talked into anything nor will he be bluffed by others. Above all, he will not allow persons who possess a dynamic temperament and whose superiority does not lie within the moral sphere to impose their ideas and advice upon him, to intimidate him, or to shake his decision.

Responsibility is not self-importance

Awareness of responsibility is an indispensable presupposition for any true moral life. By means of this basic attitude of wakefulness, everything in a man assumes its full importance, its true depth.

But one should never confuse this awareness of responsibility with a feeling of moral self-importance or with an overestimation of one's own role in the world. The responsible man must be completely inspired by the world of values and their demands; he must reverently harken to that which is objectively right, good, and beautiful; he must be inwardly free to follow always and everywhere the call of values.

Responsibility differs essentially from scrupulousness

This awareness of responsibility has nothing to do with the excessive anxiety of scrupulous persons. The scrupulous man constantly scrutinizes what he is morally obliged to do, but this does not mean that his interest in values is an extraordinary one. No, it is because he remains imprisoned within himself. Moreover, the scrupulous person is incapable of letting himself be completely carried away by the unquestionable evidence of values. He is always seeking a further guarantee than the one provided by his own insight into the value at stake.

The man who is truly awakened to his responsibility, on the contrary, remains undecided only so long as he feels he does not fully understand the claims of the value at stake. But when this certainty is reached, he feels himself secure and free.

Responsibility is a necessary basis for religion

Awareness of responsibility is a basic attitude for a religious concept of the world. The responsible man knows that he is not ruled only by an impersonal world of values, but also by a personal judge who is at the same time the Sum of all values and the one to whom he will have some day to render an account.

Consequently, this attitude, like reverence, is a basis for all religion. Its significance, like that of reverence, constancy, or fidelity, extends to every domain of life and is needed for all true knowledge, for all community life, for all artistic accomplishment, but above all for moral life, for a genuine moral personality, and for the proper relationship of creatures to the Creator. Thus one of the main aims of all education and personality formation must be to lead us to a fuller awareness of our responsibility.

4

Veracity

Truthfulness is another of the fundamental presuppositions for a person's moral life. An untruthful or mendacious person not only embodies a great moral disvalue (as does the avaricious or intemperate man) but he is crippled in his *whole* personality and in the *whole* of his moral life. Everything in him which is morally positive is threatened by his untruthfulness and even becomes doubtful. His position toward the world of values as a whole is affected at its very core.

Untruthfulness involves irreverence toward reality

The untruthful man lacks reverence toward values. He assumes a lordly position over being; he deals with it as he pleases and treats it as if it were a mere chimera, a plaything of his arbitrary pleasure. He denies recognition and response to the value which inheres in being as such, to the dignity which being possesses by its opposition to nothingness. The untruthful person does not fulfill the fundamental obligation to recognize everything that exists in its reality, not to interpret black as white, and not to deny a fact. He behaves toward being as if it did not exist. Obviously, this attitude implies an element of arrogance, of irreverence, and impertinence. To treat another person "as if he were air," to act as if this man did not exist, is perhaps the greatest evidence of disrespect and contempt. The untruthful person takes this attitude toward the world of being. A madman disregards being as being because he does not grasp it. The untruthful man grasps it as such, but refuses the response which is due to the dignity and value of being simply because it is inconvenient or disagreeable for him to do so. His disregard of being is a conscious, guilty one.

To a certain extent, a liar considers the whole world to be an instrument for his own ends. Everything which exists is but an instrument for him; when he cannot use it, then he will deal with it as nonexistent and place it in this category.

Artful liars are the most vicious

One must distinguish three different kinds of untruthfulness. The first is represented by the artful liar who sees nothing wrong in affirming the contrary of what is true when it is expedient for his aims. Here we are dealing with a man who clearly and consciously cheats and betrays other men in order to reach his aims, like Iago in Shakespeare's *Othello* or Franz Moor in Schiller's *Robbers* — although we also find in these two men a specific viciousness of intention which is not necessarily found in every liar. There also exist liars whose aims are less vicious.

Some persons practice self-deception

The second type is that of the man who lies to himself and consequently to others. He is the man who simply erases from his mind everything in his life which is difficult or disagreeable, and who not only hides his head like an ostrich, but who persuades himself that he is going to do something when he knows full well that he cannot do it. He does not want to recognize his own faults; he immediately twists the meaning of every situation which is humiliating or disagreeable for him so that it loses its sting.

The difference which is to be found between an untruthful person of this type and the hypocrite or the artful liar is evident. The untruthful person of this type practices his deception above all upon *himself*, and only indirectly upon others.

He first deceives himself and then cheats other men, half in good faith. He does not possess that consciousness of aim, that clarity which is proper to the artful liar; and in general he lacks the wickedness and cunning meanness of the artful liar. In most cases he arouses our compassion. Yet he is not without guilt, for he refuses the response due to values and to the dignity of being, and tacitly arrogates to himself an unwarranted sovereignty over being itself.

Of course, he does not have the specific impertinence toward truth of the first type of liar; some remaining respect for truth prevents him from conscious and open neglect and distortion of truth. He is afraid to take this responsibility; he lacks the courage of the hypocrite. By self-deceit he eludes the conflict between his inclinations and respect for truth. There is something specifically cowardly and feeble in his nature. In him the cunning and conscious artfulness of the liar is replaced by a more instinctive slyness.

The real liar is aware of the fact that he lies. He knows that he is ignoring reality. The untruthful person, living in self-deception, denies to himself the very fact that he is ignoring the truth in question. Because he distorts and misinterprets the facts, when he lies he is unaware of a conflict with truth.

Although a form of this untruthfulness exists also in the Pharisee (who does not see the beam in his own eye and who is wicked in the deepest sense), this type of liar is usually less responsible and generally less wicked than the artful liar. Nonetheless, the consequences of his untruthfulness are immense for his entire moral life. One can no longer take this type of person seriously. His moral action may be right in individual cases where the response to value does not involve conflict either with his pride or his concupiscence. But as soon as something disagreeable is required of him, although he will not consciously defy the call of values, he will elude it. He will take refuge in the illusion that, for one reason or another, this demand does not hold good for him, or that the demand is only an apparent one, or that he has already complied with his demand.

The inner life of such men resembles quicksand: one cannot get hold of them; they always elude one's grasp. Even though a conscious liar is, morally speaking, still more reprehensible, a conversion can more easily be brought about in him than in these self-deceivers. For these latter the inner life is affected by a greater sickness; in them evil has taken possession of a psychologically deeper level. They live in a world of illusion. Nevertheless, the untruthfulness of such men carries its share of guilt; for it could be abolished by a basic inner conversion of the will, by not shrinking from sacrifice, and by unconditional abandonment to the world of values.

Ungenuineness is a less wicked but deeper untruthfulness

In the third type of untruthfulness, the break with truth is still less reprehensible, but goes perhaps still deeper, and is reflected even more in the very being of its perpetrators. We see it in that type of ungenuine persons whose personalities are a deception, who are incapable of experiencing real joy, genuine enthusiasm, genuine love, whose every attitude is a sham and bears the stamp of pretense. These men neither want to deceive and dupe others, nor do they wish to cheat themselves; but they are unable to achieve a real and genuine contact with the world. The reason for this is that they are enclosed within themselves, always twisting their gaze back upon themselves, and in so doing they destroy the inner substance of their attitudes. The fault does not lie in their distortion of being, in their unresponsiveness to its dignity, but in a general self-centeredness which takes away the inner life of their responses and makes their personality into a sham.

These men are those shadowlike beings who are ungenuine; even though their intention is honest, their joys and sorrows are artificial. Their untruthfulness is due to the fact that all their attitudes are not really motivated by the object and are not en-flamed by contact with it, but are artificially stimulated; such attitudes pretend to conform to the object, but in reality are only phantoms without substance.

This lack of genuineness can manifest itself in different ways; above all, it can assume different dimensions. It is found, first, in the affected person whose exterior behavior, although not actually simulated, is unnatural, artificial, and untrue. It is found, secondly, in those people easily influenced by suggestion, whose opinions and convictions are imposed on them by others, and who only reaffirm what others have said without ever being truly deter-mined by the object involved. Thirdly, it is found in the exagger-ated person who works himself up in all things, in his sorrow, in his joy, in his love, in his hatred, and in his enthusiasm; he fosters these artificially because he relishes himself in those attitudes.

Ungenuineness as found in the three last-mentioned types is still less wicked than it is in him who deceives himself, but a moral life cannot be based on such a foundation. For everything — good as well as bad — is rendered invalid by such an artificial attitude. It makes everything unreal, everything a sham, a nothingness. This substantial untruthfulness is also culpable because it stems from an ultimate refusal to abandon oneself to values, from a basic attitude of pride.

The truthful man knows and respects being

The man who is really truthful is opposed to the three above mentioned types of untruthfulness. He is genuine; he cheats neither himself nor other people. Because of his deep reverence for the majesty of being, he understands the basic demand of the value which inheres in every being. (I mean by this demand the obligation of paying tribute to everything that exists, of conforming to truth in all our assertions, and of refraining from building up a world of sham and nothingness.) He takes into account the metaphysical situation of man, which grants him no omnipotence such that being must yield to his wishes as if it were a mere chimera. That is, he takes truth into account not only with regard to individual things and conditions which present themselves to his mind, but also with regard to his attitude as a man in the world. He understands the value which inheres in truth and the negative value of lies, of falsity, and of inner revolt against the world of values (and in the last account against God, the Absolute Being, the Lord of all being) that is contained in every untruth. He understands the responsibility which man as a spiritual person has in regard to truth, and which is to be found in man's power to depict being in an assertion made by him. He understands the solemnity inherent in every affirmation, for in making an affirmation one is called upon to be a witness to truth.

The truthful person places the demands of values above every subjective wish prompted by his selfishness or his comfort. He consequently abhors all self-deception. He sees the whole negative value of a cowardly flight from the objective demands of the world of values. He would rather know the most bitter truth than enjoy an imaginary happiness. The whole pointlessness of every flight into a world of unreality is clear to his eyes. He grasps the complete uselessness of self-deception, the futility of this type of behavior, the emptiness and shallowness of every untruth.

The truthful man responds genuinely to reality

Finally, the truthful man, who has a *classical* relationship with being, is the man who in his every attitude and action is genuine and true. In his soul we do not find sham attitudes; he does not embellish and puff up the experiences which he truly has; he does not twist his gaze back on himself instead of looking at the object which demands a response from him.

He is the genuine and straightforward man, the *objective* man (in the highest sense of that word). He is the man who possesses in his basic attitude true abandonment to values and who holds himself free from personal pride, so that he is not moved to arrogate to himself a position in the world other than the one which is objectively due him. Thus he neither falsifies the import of an experience, nor gives it another character than the one it possesses in reality.

Only the truthful man can develop spiritually

The truthful person does not seek compensation for his inferiority complexes. The relation which finds its expression in the words, "Humility is truth," may also be expressed conversely. The humble person alone is really truthful. The source of all ungenuineness and all untruthfulness is found in the proud desire to

be something different from what we really are. The most profound assent given to truth, to being, is the foundation for all
genuineness and truthfulness. This is often misunderstood in the
sense that the pessimist, the skeptic, the man who refuses to
recognize any higher reality than the palpable, or the fatalist who
renounces all intervention in the world and who despairs of all
progress and all development, are considered to be especially
truthful persons.

To accept this would be a complete misunderstanding. Such
persons give assent only to a segment of being and never to its
whole. They do not recognize the demand of the world of values
or the promise of development, change, and elevation of one's own
being which lies in this demand. They neglect the meaning of man
and of the world which belongs as much to being as the stone we
see lying on the ground and the air we breathe. Consequently, they
are not completely truthful, for they give assent only to the
superficial strata of being and not to its deeper and more important
strata. *Moral* transformation is always within the range of every
man. But the *non-moral* transformation of which we speak here
must take place within the framework of the person's own individuality and capacity: that is, these forms of growth must be
ontologically true and not consist in illusion or a flight into fancy.

Lying is uncharitable and a revolt against being

There exist manifold elements in the specific negative value of
a lie, the classical example of untruthfulness. First of all, in such
an affirmation there is a revolt against the dignity of being as such,
an irreverent arrogance, and a disregard of the fundamental obligation to conform to being. To lie is to misuse the quality entrusted
to us as witnesses to being, in speech, in the spoken or written
word. Secondly, we must consider the deception of other men

which is linked with a lie. To deceive another person implies a fundamental disrespect, a failure to take him seriously. It ignores the value which inheres in every man as a spiritual person and shows a disregard of the dignity of man, of the elementary right which every person possesses to know the truth. It shows, above all, a deep lack of charity and an abuse of the confidence which the other person places in us. These elements are to be found in every intentional deception practiced upon another, but, in a very special way, in a deception effected by means of a false affirmation, by a lie. For the communication by words, in its very form, implies an explicit *I-thou* relationship. This communication appeals so expressly to the basic confidence of man in man, that the lack of charity and the betrayal of the other person is still more striking and more telling in this case than in the case of a deception by means of ambiguity or misleading behavior.

Now, there are cases in which deception as such is permitted — nay, is commanded. For example, if a criminal is following us, it is permissible for us to deceive him in one way or the other about our dwelling place. Deception is commanded when we could severely harm another person either physically or morally by communicating the truth.

In the latter case, it is no lack of charity to deceive; on the contrary, it is a loving kindliness. Thus we are permitted to deceive other persons in certain given cases; in others, we are obliged to do so. But we may do this only by means of our interpretation of a given situation, not by means of a direct lie.

Veracity is a foundation for moral and religious life

Like reverence, fidelity, and the awareness of responsibility, veracity is a basis of our whole moral life. Like these other virtues, it bears a high value in itself and is also indispensable as a basic presupposition of a personality in which genuine moral values may flower in their plenitude.

This proves true in all the domains of life. Veracity is the basis for all true community life, for every relationship of person to person, for every true love, for every profession, for true knowledge, for self-education, and for the relationship of men to God. Yes, a basic element of veracity is, in a specific way, its relationship to the absolute Source of all being, God. For, in the last account, untruthfulness means a denial of God, a flight from Him. An education which does not lay emphasis on truthfulness and veracity condemns itself to failure.

5

Goodness

Goodness is the very heart of the whole reign of moral values. It is no accident that the term good means "moral value as such," and also "the specific moral quality of goodness." Among the different moral values there is none which embodies more completely the entire reign of moral values than goodness; in it we find the purest and most typical expression of the general character of moral goodness as such.

Goodness is the fruit of moral life

It is at the center of all morality and at the same time its most sublime fruit. Its central importance in the moral sphere is therefore of a completely different type from that of the fundamental attitudes previously mentioned: reverence, fidelity, awareness of responsibility, and veracity. For, apart from their own high moral value, these virtues are accepted as a presupposition for the moral life. Goodness, on the contrary, is not a presupposition, but the fruit of moral life. But goodness is not a fruit among others, such as meekness, patience, and generosity, but the fruit of fruits: that is, that in which culminates all morality in a specific way. Goodness is the queen of all virtues.

What is goodness? What do we mean when we say that a man radiates goodness? We say this of a man when he is disposed to help, when he is kindly and just, when he is ready to make sacrifices for others, when he pardons wrongs done him, when he is generous, when he is full of compassion. All these qualities are specific forms and manifestations of love. This indicates the close connection which exists between love and goodness. Love is, as it were, flowing goodness, and goodness is the breath of love.

Love is the most outspoken response to value

We have seen at the beginning that the whole moral life consists in meaningful responses to values which have been grasped — responses such as enthusiasm, admiration, joy, obedience, love. But love is, among all these responses to values, the most complete and the deepest.

First of all, one must realize that love is always an outspoken response to value. When we love somebody (whether it be a friend, a parent, a child, whether it be conjugal love or neighborly love), the beloved person always stands before us as something precious and noble in himself.

As long as someone is merely agreeable to us or only useful for our purposes, we could not love him. This does not mean that we become blind to the faults of the beloved person. But the person as a whole must stand before us as endowed with a sublime value and filled with intrinsic preciousness. Yes, that specific individuality which every man represents as a unique thought of God must reveal itself before our eyes in all its charm and beauty if we are to love him.

Love is always a response to value. In love, one responds not only with a specific word, but with the gift of one's heart, with oneself. In love, one consorts with value more closely and more deeply than in any other response such as, for example, reverence or obedience. In love, a man dwells in the values of the beloved in a completely different way. Love, in its fullest and proper meaning, addresses itself always to persons, or at least to impersonal entities which we treat as personal (as, for example, one's country).

There are responses to values (such as joy, sorrow, and enthusiasm) which are directed toward things, attitudes, and events, as well as toward persons. By their very nature, other responses to values (such as veneration, gratitude, confidence, obedience, and love) address themselves only to persons.

In the response of love to another person two fundamental elements are manifested. The affirmation of the being of the beloved one, the abandoning response to his intrinsic beauty, unfolds itself on the one hand in a longing to participate in his being, to be united with him, and on the other hand in the will to bestow happiness on him.

In love, one spiritually hastens toward the other person in order to dwell with him, to partake in him, and, on the other hand, to cover him with a mantle of goodness, to cherish him spiritually and protect him. Every love which deserves the name of love possesses these two elements, even though in a specific love, one or the other element will prevail.

Goodness is a loving attitude toward all beings

The second element is an ultimate interest in the growth and unfolding of the beloved, in his perfection and his happiness, and, in the last account, in his salvation. This envelopment of the beloved in love, is, as we have already said, pure flowing goodness.

The Art of Living

Here we find goodness in its purest manifestation. Goodness always presupposes a special attitude toward other persons, even to beings of a lower order possessing a certain analogy to persons, such as animals. Thus, it is contradistinguished from truthfulness, which responds to the value of being as such. Goodness is an attitude of response to value toward persons in general, for the goodness of a man does not limit itself to benevolent intentions toward one particular person whom he loves. When we say someone is good, we mean that he continually manifests this open benevolence, that his attitude toward every man has *a priori* this loving, generous character. For goodness, like every other virtue, is not limited to a particular momentary attitude, but is a property of man, a part of his superactual being, a basic attitude and position.

The wicked man hates goodness

There are three types of men who embody a specific antithesis to goodness: the indifferent, cold man; the hardhearted one; and the wicked one.

The latter is the man who is an enemy of values, who is ruled by a basic attitude of pride, and who lives in an impotent revolt against the world of values. He not only bluntly bypasses them, as does the sensual man, but he assails them. He would like to dethrone God; he hates the world of goodness and beauty, and all the world of light (like Alberich in the *Nibelungenring* of Richard Wagner). He is full of envy and rebellion against the world of values and against every good and happy man. He is a man like Cain, who feeds himself upon hatred. His attitude toward other men not only lacks kindliness but is expressly hostile. He wants to hurt his fellowmen and to wound them with the poison of his hatred.

I do not refer to the misanthrope who, having been disillusioned, is at war with humanity as a whole and every individual person. The misanthrope has rather turned away from mankind than turned against it; this type is more tragic than wicked. I am thinking rather of the malicious man who would like to pour out his poison everywhere, like Iago in Shakespeare's *Othello* or Pizarro in Beethoven's *Fidelio*. A specific variety of this type is the fundamentally cruel man, who enjoys the sufferings of others. Instead of the luminous harmony of goodness, we find here a somber disharmony. Instead of the warm diffusing rays of happiness and life radiated by love, one finds virulent and lacerating hatred; instead of clear, free affirmation, one finds a destroying search for nothingness, a being imprisoned in a spasm of negation.

The hardhearted man treats all things will stern coldness

We find another antithesis to goodness in the hardhearted person. He is the stern, cold man who is never moved by compassion, whose ear is deaf to all petitions, who tramples on everything without consideration, and for whom other men are mere figures placed on the chessboard of his plans. He is not a deliberate enemy of other people, but completely hard and uncharitable. In no way does this type take into account the natures of other men as spiritual persons, as sensitive and vulnerable creatures. He ignores their rights and claims as personal beings; he treats them as if they were mere objects. He represents a classical type of the pure egoist. He reminds us of certain slave dealers or of Landvogt Gassier in Schiller's *William Tell*.

Instead of the inner freedom of the charitable man, we find in him an inner compression and hardening of the heart. In place of openness and accessibility to his fellowmen, we find him closed in upon himself and impenetrable. Instead of a response to the positive value of the other's happiness and the negative value of his suffering, we find refusal of any response. Instead of solidarity with the other person (i.e., the capacity to transcend oneself in order to suffer and rejoice with others), we find total imprisonment in self, an icy and brutal gaze looking beyond others. Instead of the victorious, selfless superiority of the man who is at the service of all, we find the inferiority of the brutal superman, and instead of generous forgiveness of injustices suffered, we find relentless vengeance.

The indifferent man is neutral toward values

Finally, the antithesis to the good man is the cold, indifferent man. He is the man who bypasses his fellowmen with a blighting lack of comprehension, who lives for his own comforts and enjoyments. He, too, is a typical egoist, but he has a different complexion from the hardhearted man. He is neither hostile toward others nor brutally and unrelentingly hard, but is filled with indifference toward his fellowmen. He may be moved by fearful sights, may experience disgust and horror when facing illness, or be unable to bear the sight of blood, but all this is but a nervous reaction to an aesthetically shocking object. For he flees from awful sights and seeks pleasant scenes, while the good man hastens to help.

On the other hand, this type of man is even colder than the hardhearted man. The hardhearted man, it is true, has an icy coldness. He does not know the voice of the heart; he is heartless. Yet he does know the fire of hatred, the cold burning of vengeance and of rage. He is not indifferent. He is not invulnerable. He is familiar with the irritation caused by offenses and humiliations, but he does not know what it means to be wounded to the heart by lack of charity, injustice, and, above all, by the sufferings of our fellowmen, and other objective negative values.

The indifferent man, on the contrary, has not the sternness and brutality of the hardhearted man. He cannot even be pierced by insults; only that which is disagreeable and uncomfortable bothers him. He is not a superman like the hardhearted man; he may even be an aesthete. He is unable to share other people's feelings, for he is much too occupied with his own concerns. He is not only selfish; above all, he is egocentric. That is, he is occupied with his own feeling and moods, and his gaze is centered upon himself. The whole world is there only for his satisfaction. He is therefore incapable of deeper inward emotions; in the end everything leaves him indifferent. Instead of the warmth and ardor of the good man, empty neutrality and cool indifference reign here. We find here no inner riches or inner fecundity, only sterile poverty and fruitless emptiness. Instead of the wakefulness and openness of the good man, we find the indifferent man circumscribed and blind regarding values, and instead of the all-embracing breadth of the good man, we find in this type of man a petty narrowness.

Goodness possesses great strength

Thus we see the fundamental features of goodness: luminous harmony, inner freedom and serenity, the victorious superiority of love (which is the secret of eager and ready service), openness to the life of other men, warmth, ardor, meekness, and mildness, all-embracing breadth, wakefulness, and the capacity to grasp values. It is above all important to understand that goodness, although it is tender and meek, possesses at the same time the greatest strength. Faced with its irresistible power, with its superior security and freedom, the force of the superman is only miserable weakness and childish pretense. One should not mistake goodness for weak surrender, a surrender without resistance. The truly good man can be immovable when one tries to divert him from the right path, and when the salvation of his neighbor calls imperatively for sternness. He unshakably resists every seduction and temptation.

Good-naturedness is not goodness

One should beware of confusing good-naturedness with goodness. The good-natured man is harmless and is an appeaser; because of a certain lassitude and inertia of his nature, he lets himself be badly treated without noticing it. His amiable attitude has its source in a completely unconscious tendency of his nature. Goodness, on the contrary, flows from a conscious response of love; it is ardent wakefulness and never harmless lassitude. It is the most intense moral life, and not inertia and dullness; it is strength and not weakness. The good man does not allow himself to be made use of because he lacks the strength to resist, but he serves freely and humbles himself willingly.

Goodness is the essence of every truly moral life

In goodness there shines a light which bestows on the good person a special intellectual dignity. The truly good man is never stupid and narrow, even though he may not be gifted for intellectual activities and may even be slow intellectually. The man who is not good in any of the aforementioned ways is, in the last account, always limited and even stupid.[3] This is true even if he has produced works of great intellectual power.

---

[3] *Stupidity*, in the sense in which it is used here, is fully compatible with intellectual sharpness and cleverness, but renders a man incapable of distinguishing truth from error in all truly deep questions, which can be answered only when approached in an attitude of humility and reverence. The man whose intellectual endowment is modest, but who is good, will never fall into the same pitfalls.

Goodness, the breath and fragrance of love, is the essence of every truly moral life — yes, of every true life of the soul. Whereas the other fundamental attitudes (such as reverence, faithfulness, responsibility, and veracity) respond to the world of values as a whole, goodness not only responds to this world of values, but is, so to speak, the reflection of the whole world of values in the person. Goodness speaks in the voice and in the name of this world of values.

What has been said of love applies to goodness as well: "He who does not love abides in death."[4] In its mysterious strength, goodness shakes the world to its very foundations; it bears on its forehead the sign of victory over wickedness and disorder, over all hatred and all unfeeling coarseness.

[4] 1 John 3:14.

6

Communion

The great French writer Léon Bloy once wrote "there is but one real sadness: not to be a saint." On the other hand Gabriel Marcel says that "there is but one sadness: to be alone."

At first sight, these two assertions are completely different, but if we care to penetrate more deeply into what Gabriel Marcel so aptly calls the "mysteries of Being," we shall see that there is a profound, although subtle, link between them. It is the nature of this link that we shall presently examine.

Sin severed man's relation to God and to other men

The saint is precisely he who lives in constant and intimate communion with God, he who does not allow anything or anyone to separate him from God, he who victoriously links to God everything happening to him, sickness or health, poverty or wealth, infamy or fame.

The saint is the person who has conquered the isolation which is created by sin — namely, Original Sin, which has severed the relationship existing between God and man and, as a consequence, the relationship existing between man and man. When Adam and Eve were exiled from the earthly paradise, they were exiled *together*, and yet this seeming togetherness should not blind us to their *isolation* from one another.

Original Sin has created a state of separation between man and God, and the whole work of redemption seeks to mend this rupture and to reestablish the triumph of communion.

Communion is not fusion

In order to shed light upon this, let us for a moment contemplate man's nature. Man is the most perfect substance known to us through experience, for he is the most perfect individual that we know. Man can never cease to be himself and become a mere part of something else.

It is quite conceivable that man should cease to exist at the moment of death; but it is thoroughly inconceivable that he could continue to exist, while vanishing as an individual self and being *absorbed* as a part into another larger reality.

On the other hand, and precisely on account of this selfhood, man is destined to enter into communion with other persons; and it is in and through this communion that he fulfills himself. In order to understand the nature of this fundamental truth, we must liberate ourselves from a prejudice deeply rooted in certain intellectual circles. This prejudice consists in taking for granted that fusion is the prototype of communion.

We cannot insist sufficiently upon the abyss separating the two: when two drops of water fuse and become one, we cannot speak of communion between them, because they have no knowledge that they have become united. Knowledge is the essential presupposition for communion.

Knowledge and love are the greatest forms of communion

So we see that precisely because man is a more perfect substance than any other being known to us through experience, he
is capable of entering into communion with other persons. The
two great forms of communion are knowledge and love. In knowledge, I spiritually turn toward another person, and then through
questioning and answering a spiritual contact is established between us which is unthinkable and impossible in the impersonal
world. The climax of communion between persons is reached in
love, as we shall see later on.

Now that we are more keenly conscious of man's calling to
enter into communion with other personal beings, we are ready to
understand why man suffers when he fails to attain it. The anxiety
and the despair which are manifested upon so many human faces
are expressions of the sorrow a human being feels when he discov-
ers himself to be isolated, to be thrown back upon himself, incapable of establishing a communion with another. Maybe it is not
exaggerated to say that the drama of the society in which we live
lies in the fact that we put the greatest weight on *social* contacts,
while living in a tragic isolation.

Solitude takes many forms

Let us now examine briefly the various types of solitude which
can be found in human life. First, there is a type of solitude which
is created by the fact that I happen to be completely and totally
alone, physically speaking. There are situations in which this
lonesomeness is experienced as a relief: for example, when I am
with other persons who are cold and distant toward me. As soon
as I am alone once more, I feel that I can breathe again. It is clear
that to be alone under such circumstances is a blessing, but we

should not infer erroneously that it is always a blessing. Let us recall that solitary confinement is a traditional form of punishment and a particularly refined one, for it throws man back upon himself, forcing him, so to speak, to knock his head against his own limitations.

To be alone can also be linked to a particular type of anxiety. Suppose that I find myself in a great physical danger, isolated on top of a mountain. Suddenly I discover that there is another man sharing my predicament. This gives me a feeling of elation and relief. We shall find some way out; we shall help one another. But quite apart from the possible help that the presence of another human being can give me, the fact that I am no longer alone in the great, cold, impersonal universe creates a totally new situation, a situation in which the possibility of communicating, of talking, warms up the cool objectivity of a world which was made for human presence. Suddenly, I am transported into an *intrapersonal* space. Let us recall Dante's immense relief, when after a night passed in qualms, he perceived Vergil (not knowing that it was he):

> Have pity upon me, I imploring cried,
> whether thou be of shades or real men.

Physical loneliness can also make me realize the victorious transcendence of my love for another person; for even though I am separated from the one I love, I feel that no human power can truly sever the bond uniting us. On the other hand, closely linked to this experience of victory is the acute suffering resulting from the separation itself; we only need recall the deep words of Keats to his friend Fanny Brawne: "The very air I breathe is unhealthy without you."

But we now come to another type of solitude, which is completely different from the first; it is the solitude I experience when

I am *with* other persons in some sort of social gathering. The fact that one can be totally isolated in the company of other people is proved by innumerable experiences. Man's transcendence over animals, which can be shown in so many ways, is also evidenced by the fact that animals are content with the mere physical presence of other animals. For man, the physical presence of others severed from some sort of spiritual contact is a refined form of suffering. While reading Gabriel Marcel's plays, we have been struck by the fact that his characters complain of *solitude*, and that these are precisely married people living in apparent communion with one another. In such cases, one can truly speak of a *solitary crowd,* of people thrown together while remaining in hopeless isolation. Some cocktail parties we have attended bore all the marks of this deceptive communion, this social lie. There is a way of greeting people in which the content of the words used ("I am delighted to see you") is formally denied by the tone of anonymity used. One feels very strongly that the person "delighted to see you" has not focused upon you for a single moment, has treated you as a number, as an object, as a thing, and in no way as an individual person.

Reverence makes possible communion between persons

We should realize that our highly mechanized society constitutes a very real threat to human relationships. More and more we are getting accustomed to seeing other persons as numbers in a multitude and not as real selves, as unique, irreplaceable individuals. From this point of view we can appreciate the depth of Kierkegaard's remark when he says that God does not know crowds; He only knows individuals.

I once received a compliment which I treasure to this very day: someone said "you are the first person I have met in my life who has been willing to listen to me." This remark was a surprise, for I remembered that after listening to my friend, I was at a loss for an answer to his problem. But he did not expect an answer at all; he just wanted to know that there was someone willing to listen, willing to take his problems seriously. Thanks to this person, I understood the nature of one fundamental failure in human relationships: the lack of *reverence* with which we tend to approach other persons. I noted earlier that reverence is the mother of all virtues. It is also the mother of all human relationships.

Problems are essentially different from mysteries

At this point a distinction borrowed from Gabriel Marcel will help us understand one of the great dangers threatening communion. According to Marcel, we should make a fundamental distinction between *problems* and *mysteries*. A *problem*, he tells us, is an objective difficulty and has two main features or peculiarities: first, it is totally unrelated to myself; it is objective in the scientific sense given to this term. Second, it can be solved and, once solved, it ceases to be a problem at all. It is like a knot that has been untied.

A *mystery*, on the other hand, is intimately connected with myself, so much so that I cannot approach it adequately without realizing that I myself am involved in it.

Moreover, a mystery can never be solved in the sense of ceasing to be a mystery. An example will illustrate this point. There is evil in the world. According to Marcel, we are all too prone to see evil as an accident happening in the complicated machine of the universe; we interpret it as a cog missing in a complex wheel, and put the blame on the maker of the universe for having failed to engineer it properly. On the other hand, we look for a solution to this problem, and the most threatening solution man has come across so far is communism, for communism claims to be the one, final solution to all human problems. Communism claims to have discovered that the cog missing is an adequate understanding of the sphere of economics. Once wealth becomes the exclusive possession of the state, all human difficulties will be solved, for everyone will receive according to his productivity and his needs. The problem is solved, and the results are well-organized concentration camps.

In fact, evil is not a problem, but much rather a mystery in which I myself am personally involved; for it is useless to fight evil in the world, be it injustice or wickedness, if I fail to discover the roots of the same disease in my own soul. We must, however, add to this distinction of Gabriel Marcel the observation that the term *mystery* can apply to very different things.

There are different kinds of mysteries

First, there is mystery in the religious sense; this is what surpasses the rational sphere as such, namely, the suprarational which we can only embrace in faith. Examples of this type of mystery are the Holy Trinity or the transubstantiation in the Eucharist.

Second, there are rational antinomies which we cannot solve with our reason, such as the coexistence of evil with the infinite goodness of God. They are not suprarational, but remain enigmatic for our reason, at least during our earthly existence.

Third, there are things which I cannot solve practically, things which are not to be changed by any plan, by any human effort, such as evil on this earth. Here the attempt to solve them with human regulations leads to making them worse, as we just saw in the case of communism, or any terrestrial messianism.

Fourth, we can call a "mystery" something which, because of its depth and richness, is inaccessible to a purely rational penetration in a geometrical fashion. In this sense the human person is a mystery; love is a mystery; beauty is a mystery. Although they are not suprarational, although they in no way contain antinomies, these mysteries escape the kind of rational explanation which is to be found in logic or mathematics. They also are so deep that we can never exhaust them with our knowledge.

We must approach other persons as mysteries

In this sense, communion with other persons is a mystery. It is this latter sense of mystery versus problems which applies to our specific context. Marcel tells us that philosophical mysteries cannot be solved, but we can shed light upon them.

Now, we are often tempted to see other persons as problems, and as we must live with them, we are eager to get some "tips" on how to deal with them. For example, we hear that a person with whom we will have to work has a very high idea of himself and of his accomplishments. We immediately infer that in order "to get on his good side" we shall have to pay him compliments.

Now, it is not illegitimate to try to get on someone's good side, but it does become illegitimate the moment we reduce the other person to the level of a puzzle, without any reverence for his own true self; it becomes illegitimate when we view him as a complex machine whose secret code we must discover. Once we discover it, we can work it at will and elicit any reaction that we please.

It is not difficult to see that this attitude is fearfully irreverent and does not imply the slightest trace of respect for the other person's individuality.

Isolation may be self-inflicted

It is, however, also possible that one is fully responsible for his own isolation from others. If I make myself the absolute center of the universe, view everything and everyone exclusively from the point of view of the possible advantage or disadvantage that they can bring me, I lock myself up in myself, and should not marvel if I find myself in total isolation.

In his *Divine Comedy* Dante distinguished between the two forms of isolation we have just mentioned. In Hell, which is the homeland of isolation, the heretics suffer from absolute loneliness, each one of them buried in the tomb of his own errors; whereas another type of punishment consists in togetherness without any love, where the very presence of another person who hates you adds to your sufferings.

Fusion is an insuperable obstacle to communion

Finally, we can speak of a type of solitude created by radical nondualism. This latter position is typical of some Oriental doctrines which claim that in fact everything is one; it is only cosmic illusion to believe that there is multiplicity. Ultimately, all things will return to the one unchanging metaphysical principle which is the only true reality. It might be argued that this attitude flows from an ardent, if unconscious, desire to reach communion. Be that as it may, absolute metaphysical fusion does not conquer communion, but actually makes it impossible. For a part is not and cannot be in communion with the whole; it is absorbed by it.

Self-centered mediocrity is an obstacle to communion

Let us now turn to a closer analysis of the obstacles which must be overcome for communion to be established between two persons. Once again let us borrow a key idea from Gabriel Marcel. He tells us in various works that each man has the tendency to remain imprisoned in the narrow circle of his self-interest and his own petty selfishness. This constitutes what he calls the *moi*, which can be compared to a closed monad "without windows," to quote Leibniz. But, Gabriel Marcel, tells us, man has other possibilities; he can also break free from the self-centeredness of his own egotism, and open up simultaneously to a different dimension of his own being. This is the discovery of the *I* in myself which faces a *thou*, that is, another person with whom I am in communion.

The birth of the *I* in myself implies a glorious victory over my own narrowness and selfishness. This victory is preceded by a battle, and it is precisely this battle against one's selfishness which many people are not willing to undertake. This is why many men prefer the comfortable nest of their own selfishness to the adventure of breaking open the doors of their self in order to meet another.

Men might reason, moreover, that every communion implies a risk and that by accepting it, we also open the door to sufferings, disillusions, and possible bitterness. Is it not safer, more reasonable to remain peacefully imprisoned in oneself? The love of mediocrity, so deeply rooted in man's nature, usually puts on the garments of reasonableness: "What can we hope to reach? Men cannot truly find one another. I do not wish to expose myself to bitterness and disillusion. I do no one any harm by remaining within myself."

The higher something ranks, the greater is the risk which it implies. The great gift of freedom of will implies the risk of sin. But without this risk, moral values would not be possible. Moral goodness ranks so high in God's eyes that He did not shun the risk included in freedom.

Granted, risks taken because of sheer boldness, even though no high values are at stake, are an outgrowth of self-assurance. These risks should not be taken. But to shun a high good, a great gift of God, only because a risk may be connected with it is completely erroneous.

We must remain open to communion

Communion is a gift and no effort on my part can ever achieve it; but I should be ready, "open," as Gabriel Marcel puts it. That is, I should have the inner readiness to accept communion if it should be offered to me. If I decide, in principle, that I shall refuse whatever gift will be granted me, I make a final option for my own mediocrity and finitude. I settle down in the stifling narrowness of my selfishness and reject the offer given me to enter a world in which, while losing my *moi*, I conquer myself.

It is noteworthy to remark that man is so very much made for communion that when he fails to attain it with other human beings, he tries to reach it with animals. Numerous cases could be cited of people who give all their affection to animals. This "love" is usually linked to a marked misanthropy. I recall an elderly woman who lived in our neighborhood for many years, and whose affection for her dog made her the center of our neighborhood's interest. She used to talk to it all the time, saying things such as "You, at least, won't abandon me; you'll remain faithful to me." Granted that a dog's faithfulness is something remarkable, granted that a dog will never abandon or betray you, we should never forget that the faithfulness of a dog can never be more than a dog's faithfulness.

Not long ago, while browsing through *Ring of Bright Water*, I came upon a passage in which the author tells us that when his otter died, he missed him more than he would have missed most of the people he knew, for he said "no one has trusted me as totally as my otter had." There is an element of tragedy hidden under these words.

Human communion implies a risk because it is based upon freedom and because we can never be given a mathematical exterior guarantee that it will not lead to disillusions. But as we saw, all great things in life imply a risk: the creation of works of art, birth, life, friendship, marriage.

Functionalism threatens communion

Another reason, I believe, why communion so often fails to be reached in our society is due to the importance granted to our work, our function in society. My students tell me that, from their early youth on, the whole accent of education is put on the question: What will you *do* to earn a living? Little is said (if anything at all) about what one will *be* as a person. Little by little, we accustom ourselves to seeing ourselves as nurse, as secretary, as teacher, and so forth, and this vision colors strongly the formation of our personality. There used to be such a thing as a typical telephone operator; she possessed a remarkably empty politeness. Her "I am sorry" when she gave you the wrong connection was impeccably correct and remarkably unremorseful. She seemed to be playing a social role, and this social role seemed to have so marked her personality that if ever she got married and burned the dinner, her "I am sorry" spoken to her husband might well have had the very same tone that she had while answering the phone.

The other day someone called me on the phone, and just her way of greeting revealed the nature of her errand: she was heading a hospital fundraising drive and asked me to head the drive in our house. It struck me as tragic that someone should become such a "hospital drive" type that she could be identified by her very function.

This *functionalism*, if we may call it so, is a grave threat to interpersonal relationships because it actually prevents a person from discovering himself and knowing who he is. Kierkegaard was aware of this danger, and reminds us eloquently that a man should be a man before he is, let us say, a professor.

Being is more important than doing

Our society is severely endangered by this impersonalism. In order to fight it, we should become aware of the threat it constitutes in our own personal life. We must also realize that we should *respect* ourselves, God's image in our souls. In our society so much emphasis is placed upon a person's accomplishments that we are finally led to overlook completely what a person *is*.

What I have in mind is typified in the well-known phrase "He is a self-made man," a phrase which incites us to look up to the person whose performances are so remarkable that in fact he has succeeded in doing something that cannot be done: namely, to make himself.

Inferiority complexes arise mostly because we make an unhealthy comparison between the accomplishments of another person and ourselves. But how little attention is paid to the other person's *being,* his kindness, generosity, humility, patience? The less we respect ourselves as persons made in God's image, the more we shall be led to identifying ourselves with our social role, our job, our accomplishments, real or imaginary. We are led to believe that success in life lies primarily in our ability to bring *credentials,* and yet who would dream of saying to another person "I love you because you are the most efficient secretary I have met in my life" or "because you are the teacher who best organizes his material"? Love is not concerned with a person's accomplishments; it is a response to a person's *being.*

This is why a typical word of love is to say "I love you, because you are as you are." God loved us prior to our doing anything, and this very love makes man lovable. This lovableness, which is ours without our meriting it, is something which we must accept with humility and which in fact constitutes the indispensable basis for further accomplishments.

The Art of Living

God's love is a basis for communion with others

Now we come to the most important part of our topic. The basic antithesis to all torments created by solitude is shelteredness in the love of God, in communion with Christ. But apart from this, our trust in God's love is also the basis of any true communion with other human persons. We shall come back to the fundamental role of shelteredness in God's love for true communion with human persons later on. Here we need only stress its influence on the human fear of taking risks. Few are those whose life is based upon this shelteredness in God's love, and as a result, people fear an encounter with another person who might reject them.

Communion is different from social acceptance

This leads to another idea whose role in our society can hardly be overestimated: the idea that the most important thing in our relationship to other people is to be socially *accepted*. Granting that to be in communion with other persons is of central value and importance in human life, we must beware of confusing this deep human experience with conviviality, with a harmless, superficial being together which, in the best of cases, creates the illusion of communion but is in fact separated from it by an abyss. The stress put in our society on this superficial togetherness is such that a child who has no television in his home feels ashamed and excluded from those who do and with whom he cannot share television fads.

How often can we say that the price to be paid for being accepted is to make serious compromises such as lowering one's moral standards or giving up centrally important ideas which are officially labeled as "old-fashioned" or "sissy"? Quite apart from the compromises which a person might have to make in order to be accepted, the important point is that the person whose whole ideal is to be accepted puts on "garments" which are not his own and which will probably lead to a total betrayal of his own true self, of his own true personality and inner calling. The ludicrous side of this regrettable tendency lies in the fact that actually it is a small, dynamic minority which enforces its views on a gullible and weak majority, who believe themselves to be "convinced," while in fact they have only yielded.

It is easy to see that such an attitude of shallow conformism actually destroys the basis for any real communion between human beings and nourishes a life so artificial, so alien to the deep roots of the self, that the seeds of a possible communion will wither and die before they are given a chance to blossom.

Dullness of spirit is a perennial threat to communion

Enough has been said about the difficulties of attaining communion with another human person. Let us now examine the obstacles lying in the way of those who have been granted a real communion with another. We should not limit to physical phenomena the power exercised by the law of gravity; it also applies to our spiritual life. We grow wings (to quote Plato) when we fall in love and are granted a profound contact with another person! It is as if we see the world with new eyes, as if we have awakened from a slumber to a full awareness. And yet, after a while, we seem to get used to the incredible gift granted to us, the gift of starting to *live* truly (to quote Gabriel Marcel) instead of just vegetating. After a while, we become more engrossed in what is so erroneously called *real life*; everyday preoccupations wrap us up more and more, and little by little, we fall back into our old self, into our *moi*. Whether we recall Shakespeare's lines "Men are April when they woo; December when they wed" or think of the parable of the

Sower[5] or they all point to the same thing: the danger of falling back to sleep, the danger of taking things for granted, and of forgetting that to receive a great gift implies the responsibility of caring for it, of sheltering it, and protecting its growth and development. This danger is all the more serious because people do not realize how dangerous it is. They reason that the time of romance must come to an end: the honeymoon cannot last forever; now it is time to go back to serious life. Love is more serious than work

This may be the most ominous mark characterizing our epoch: namely, the tendency to see love, marriage, and friendship as relaxations from work, which is seen as the more serious part of life. Alas, we are far from remembering that work was meant to be a punishment, inflicted upon Adam after Original Sin. Apart from our relation to God, marriage and friendship should be at the very center of our lives. Work is a necessity, a duty, but something whose importance cannot be compared to the value of family life. It is a very serious perversion to view professional work as the serious part of life and family life as a relaxation. No, the time I spend with my loved ones is not the time to relax and take it easy, but rather the moment to put on my festival garment, the moment to accomplish a real lifting up of my heart. It is the moment to realize that my love for another person is, humanly speaking, the precious pearl of my life, and that I must prepare myself for every encounter with my beloved with the same grateful recollection I experienced at the moment of first falling in love. To quote Keats again: "Love is no plaything." It is a remnant from earthly paradise and it must be treated accordingly.

We should oppose the trend so prevalent in the modern world which allows family life to recede more and more into the background, until we can say there is no more family and no more life.

---

[5] Mark 4; Matt. 13; Luke 8.

Partners in marriage must remain independent persons

The same spiritual laziness can manifest itself in another direction. Marriage creates a unity between the two partners which is a unity of souls, but also a unity of life. But we have seen that the type of unity proper to communion presupposes that the two partners remain independent persons. Now when dulled by habit, life in common can lead to a *false identification* of the two persons. Gabriel Marcel has shed light upon the nature of this subtle danger in one of his plays called *Other People's Hearts*. The theme is a marriage certainly based upon love, but one in which the husband more and more considers his wife as part of himself. He no longer considers it necessary to discuss plans with her or inquire into her wishes, because, as he puts it, he feels he can take for granted that they are identical to his. She feels that she is being treated as a thing, not as a person, and suffers deeply from this lack of reverence on her husband's part.

This danger is so subtle that instead of being viewed as a threat to communion, it is rather interpreted as an expression of the unshakeable union which exists between husband and wife.

To use Marcel's terminology, instead of having a real *we communion* (which implies the *I* and the *Thou*), all that is left is an inflated ego, in this case that of the husband. He treats his wife as a possession, as a thing; he no longer treats her as a person.

Disillusionment is a threat to communion

The greatest threat concerning communion is to be found in failures of the loved one. Falling in love is essentially to be granted a vision of the beauty of another person's individuality. This vision fills us with reverence and simultaneously with a powerful attraction for the object whose beauty has been perceived. Literally, to love another person means to see his beauty, to discover the secret of his personality. This vision as we have called it, is so convincing that we say, "I shall never forget it."

Unfortunately, everyday life puts its dust on everything. The shortcomings, mistakes, and imperfections of the loved one come to the fore, and often blur my perception of his beauty. The great temptation is to say then: "Love has made me blind. I projected so many perfections into my loved one, but now that I have a second look at him, I see clearly that much of what I attributed to him is sheer illusion."

Pride blinds us to the faults of our beloved

The idea that love is blind is almost as old as philosophy, for we already find it propounded in Plato's *Symposium* by one of the guests of the banquet. Granted that it is quite possible for a person to be totally blind to the faults of a beloved person, the question is whether it is love that blinds him.

We say of a mother who obstinately refuses to see the faults of her child that "she is blinded by love." That the mother is blinded is clear, but that it is love which is responsible for her blindness is quite another matter. Is it not more correct to say that it is *pride* which blinds her to her child's mistakes? It is as if the mother said to herself, "My child cannot have these faults, because she is *my* child; how should *my* child be able to do such a thing?"

We see clearly that this mother views her child as does someone with an inflated ego, and for *this* reason: it is unbearable for her to see and admit the child's mistakes. Far from being love which blinds her, it is rather the very imperfection of her love that allows her pride to take over. It is as if this mother said to herself, "If truly my child possesses these faults and shortcomings, then I shall no longer love her."

Love sees the beloved clearly

True love, on the contrary, sees with illuminating clearness the image of the loved one, what he is called upon to be, what he is in God's eyes; and simultaneously, against the background of this vision of beauty, the lover sees that his beloved is still far from realizing it. The loved one is *in statu viae*, on the way to becoming it; he has not yet fulfilled himself.

It should now be clear that true love pitilessly sees the faults and shortcomings of the loved one, but interprets these faults differently. At this point, I must refer to a feature of love elaborated by Dietrich von Hildebrand.

Love sees what the beloved is meant to be

Indeed, a fundamental characteristic of love is that all the good qualities of the beloved are considered to be a valid expression of his true self, whereas his faults are interpreted as an unfaithfulness toward his true self. To say "this is not his true self," when the beloved commits some fault, is a typical word of love.[6]

Whereas we usually consider the values and the disvalues in a person to be equally characteristic of him, to belong equally to his self, it is typical of love, which implies a response to the beauty of this individual person, to consider all the disvalues as noncharacteristic of him, as an unfaithfulness toward his true self, a failure truly to be himself.

This distinguishes all kinds of love from a neutral, so-called "objective" attitude toward other persons. The psychologist called as an expert in court will balance or weigh with one another

---

[6] This point is elaborated in Dietrich von Hildebrand, *Man and Woman* (Manchester, N.H.: Sophia Institute Press, 1992).

positive and negative qualities of the defendant. The lover, on the contrary, will consider the positive as the expression of his real, authentic self, and the negative as betrayal of his true self, a denial, a falling away from it.

This is the *credit* which love and love alone gives to the beloved. This credit is also a specific mark of love of neighbor. Here love responds to the ontological value of the person, to his character as an image of God, seeing him in the light of the *similitudo Dei*, that is, the sanctification which he is called upon to attain. Every fault is thus seen as a betrayal of his character as an image of God, an infidelity, an apostasy from his true self.

Thus love does not overlook the faults of the beloved and is in no way blind toward them; but the lover approaches them in a completely different way. It must be emphasized that the approach of love is in reality much more objective, much more true, than the one of the neutral observer. It is not only more objective, but is even the only objective and adequate approach, because it alone is true to the nature of the person. This credit is a great gift which the lover bestows on the beloved. It implies an element of hope which is an incredible comfort and help for the beloved.

Love has faith in the goodness of the beloved

Yet that is not the only credit granted by love. Love also interprets everything in the best light, as long as it does not reveal itself as definitely negative. There are so many things in man which can be interpreted in very different ways, so many deeds, attitudes, and sayings which are in themselves neither morally good nor evil, neither beautiful nor ugly, but which gain their meaning and characteristic only when seen against the background of this special individual person. Whereas it is a typical mark of malevolence and hatred to be on the lookout for the other person's mistakes, and consequently to interpret everything in him in the worst possible light, it is a basic element of love that one has the readiness to interpret everything in the best possible light, as long as it is not univocally negative. This credit implies an element of believing in the other person.

It may precisely be this *faith* which will give the loved one the courage to fight against his own frailties. As a matter of fact, we believe that certain persons never muster the strength to fight their mistakes because they have never met anyone willing to believe in them. Faith is an essential element of love, and he who stops loving because the true image of his beloved is momentarily covered up, did not truly love in the first place.

Hope is an essential element in love

Because love is essentially related to faith, it is also intimately linked to *hope*, the hope that the one I love will one day become what I know he is called upon to be. Hope is patient. Whereas the impatient man sets deadlines and, when they are not met, falls into revolt and despair, the true lover gets impatient precisely because his hope is so much alive that he trusts that what is not accomplished today can and will take place tomorrow.

Love is so much linked to hope that it will never force another person into becoming what I know he should become, but it will patiently and reverently accept the rhythm of development proper to another person, while trusting all the time that he will come to be what I know he should be.

Charity must permeate every love

We now see that the three supernatural virtues of faith, hope, and love also give us a key to an understanding of natural human love. This confirms a basic Platonic principle: namely, we can only discover the true meaning of the world in which we live if we keep our eyes fixed above this world. Yet we must go even further. All natural categories of love (such as parental or filial love, friendship or spousal love) can fully reach what their love aspires to only when they are transformed by Christ. It is only when the spirit of charity permeates the respective category of love with its glorious breath of sublime goodness and heroic self-donation that love can be true to its own essence.

This transformation in no way erases the specific character of each type of love. On the contrary, all the typical features of the respective category of love will be more perfectly unfolded when this transformation has taken place. Pope Pius XII stated this beautifully when he said that "God with His love neither destroys nor changes nature, but perfects it." Clearly, there is only one solution to solitude — the scourge of our times — and this solution is Christ.

7

Hope

One of the criticisms which Gabriel Marcel levels at traditional philosophy is that it has failed to include in its definition of man man's capacity to despair. Man, he tells us, is a being capable of severing his metaphysical link with existence, his umbilical link with being.

Only rational beings are capable of despair

Obviously, an unintelligent being could not despair of any-thing. Gabriel Marcel is therefore taking his point of departure from man as a rational animal; but he challenges Aristotelian philosophy on the ground that it gives man a false metaphysical security in calling him a rational animal. This definition may lead man to feel sheltered in the consciousness of his own rationality.

Despair is linked to the consciousness of a metaphysical calling, a metaphysical destiny left unfulfilled. The despairing man says "it is too late," and this "too late" carries with it an implicit denial of God's creative power, a forgetting that He who has created us out of nothingness has not abandoned us and remains a Creator. "Too late" ignores the eternal renewal of the generous creativity of God.

Without immortality, every human existence contemplated as such must end in despair, for death is, visibly speaking, the last word. This pitiless, terminal character of death as the apparent last word of human existence is particularly striking if we think of the death of a beloved person as a possible source of despair.

Unconscious despair is widespread

It is one of Kierkegaard's merits to have put his finger on man's potential for despair. Anticipating the psychoanalytic stress on the unconscious, he tells us in *Sickness unto Death* that one of the most widespread types of despair, and one of the most desperate ones, is a despair unconscious of itself. Numerous are the men who go through life not knowing where they come from, not knowing where they are going, and who seem to be floating through life, apparently unconcerned about their origin or their destiny.

Of course, they know that one day they will have to die; of course, they know that life is insecure and uncertain. But they remain on a level of consciousness where these metaphysical menaces are carefully veiled in an abstractness and insubstantiality which make them look harmless and unreal.

To refer to Martin Heidegger, these people will speak of death with the same coolness with which they mention the law of gravity; it is clear that "one" must die, but this "one" is never identified with self. They are so afraid of a metaphysical confrontation with death that if they had to do so they would probably commit suicide immediately rather than be forced to live with such a threatening prospect.

These people sail through life, apparently satisfied, gloating over each small enjoyment bestowed upon them, eagerly looking forward to what tomorrow will bring. And yet as far as they are concerned, there might not be a tomorrow at all.

Living for pleasure breeds despair

Kierkegaard has characterized this as the tragedy of living for pleasure. But pleasure, he tells us, is by its very nature timebound. It begins in time, reaches its climax, and declines. It is, in principle, possible to imagine an eternal succession of pleasures, one rapidly succeeding another; but it is inconceivable that one pleasure should be eternal. But if it is of the essence of pleasure to be in time and time floats constantly and continually forward, then a life centered exclusively on pleasures is a life menaced by despair. For, to quote Kierkegaard again, "If the moment is everything, the moment is nothing."

Simultaneously — and this is important — every pleasure, small as its duration may be, gives one just enough "fuel" to long for the next pleasure. It keeps pushing one forward in a state of restlessness and tension that makes it very difficult to meditate on the hopelessness of this state.

Pleasures give less than they promise

St. Augustine, whose genius has anticipated so many of the existential philosophies, remarks pointedly that while it is characteristic of earthly pleasures that they give less than they promise, the very reverse is true of eternal beatitude; our strongest desires can never give us any adequate foretaste of the joy that will be granted us.

This "fuel" which every pleasurable experience gives us should be analyzed more accurately. We long for a particular pleasure; it takes hold of our attention to such an extent that we seem to care for nothing else. We eagerly anticipate its enjoyment which, in this moment, seems to become an "all." But rare are the cases in which the actual enjoyment lives up to the promise that it has given us.

Oftentimes, the realization of this pleasure is accompanied by a note of disillusion, small as it may be. To illustrate the point, we need only observe children who desperately wish to obtain a toy. They can talk about nothing else; they are willing to make strenuous efforts or extraordinary sacrifices to have their wish fulfilled. Upon its realization, they anticipate heaven; they expect a total and long-lasting change in their lives. But after a few days of feverish possession, their interest seems to decline; the glow that threw this particular object into relief seems to vanish, and soon afterwards, the object once so passionately desired is incapable of affording its possessor any particular or outstanding satisfaction.

The interesting fact, however, is that this experience, although consciously registered, will in no way change or alter the passionate anticipation of the next pleasure-giving object. Indeed, if one were reminded of the disillusion experienced in the past, this reminder would immediately be drowned in a powerful whirl of rationalizations which would explain away the strength of this objection.

Pleasure-seeking can become a form of slavery

There is a deep-seated wish within man to *trust* the power of pleasures, to believe that in the long run they will be capable of yielding to us a state of delight that can be had for the asking and retained at will.

So the very hopelessness of finding in pleasures a key to happiness goes hand in hand with another hopelessness: the one of liberating oneself from the chains of this enslavement, for the enjoyment of every pleasure is psychologically linked to the promise of another pleasure.

It is important to note that the very immanence of the round of pleasures leads men to believe that there is no hope of transcendence for them, and this throws men back still more brutally upon the crumbs of satisfaction that pleasure can yield.

It is, I believe, this immanent law of the pleasurable which has led Kierkegaard to say that man can regain his liberty only by means of a leap — that is, a breaking away from the encircling prison of the pleasurable to another sphere of human existence, to another depth of its possibilities.

Captivity to pleasure is a form of despair

Many human beings find themselves in this captivity, a captivity whose hopelessness is *despair*. And yet, most people, while finding themselves in this desperate state, are not conscious of their own despair for the very reasons we have mentioned above: the ostrich policy of not facing one's own despair, of not calling it by its right name, and simultaneously, the subtle promise contained in every pleasure that another pleasure will lead to some sort of fulfillment.

These men who repress their despair (to use psychoanalytic terminology) by immersing themselves in the turmoil of pleasures behave like persons whose marriage is profoundly unhappy. On the surface, they strike us as contented, successful individuals; and in point of fact, they can walk along life's paths rather cheerfully as long as they are not brought face-to-face with the tragedy of their situation, as long as they are not aware of the abysmal gap between a truly happy marriage and their present situation. This escapism is one of the most subtle defense mechanisms which nature has produced. But this defense mechanism is a two-edged sword, for the very protection it affords makes it nearly impossible for the person in question to liberate himself and take the leap to a higher sphere of existence.

There is a form of charity which consists in helping another person not to discover his own misery, as long as the discovery of the same cannot be coupled with its remedy. Descartes has already wisely remarked in his *Discourse* that a man, dissatisfied with his house, will patiently wait before he tears it down until another, more hospitable house should be ready to receive him. Similarly, it is a risky affair to make another person conscious of his despair, if one is incapable of simultaneously giving him a ray of hope.

Yet, it should be clear that this type of metaphysical "hide and seek" constitutes a pitiable state, one whose tragedy lies in the very betrayal of man's innermost possibility: his being made for God. Let us quote the words of St. Augustine: "For Thou hast made us for Thyself and our hearts are restless till they rest in Thee."

Consciousness of despair can itself cause greater despair

Kierkegaard tells us that there is another type of man who has become conscious of the hopelessness of constant pleasures and its accompanied self-centeredness. He has reached the stage of conscious despair, but the very consciousness of his despair plunges him into a deeper despair, which can lead him to envying the man who does not know how unhappy he is. Consciousness of one's own despair constitutes a real advantage over what Kierkegaard termed "unconscious despair," for this consciousness is necessary in order to take the leap that will bring one beyond the fangs of despair.

But from another point of view, consciousness of one's despair, coupled with a new form of despair over one's despair, constitutes a particularly cruel situation. The peculiarity of this form of despair is to be found in an extreme lucidity toward one's past. The person in question sees with pitiless clearness the hopelessness of his situation, the dead alley into which a life centered exclusively upon the merely subjectively satisfying necessarily leads. He sees, moreover, with enviable clarity that man need not despair, that the road of transcendence lies open to him. However, simultaneously by some sort of perversion, he claims that this road, open to all men, is closed to *him*. He will tell you that had he been a bit younger, had circumstances been slightly different, he could have found his way toward hope. But, given his concrete situation, it should be clear that the word *hope* remains meaningless to him.

The despairing cry of this man is "for *me* it is too late." While realizing the pitiless limits of time, he simultaneously declares that the Creator of time cannot possibly *redeem time* in his case. The attitude of such a man, while preserving the appearance of humility, reverses the roles between Creator and creatures; and instead of praying with the Psalmist "My lots are in Thy hands"[7] he seems to say "*Your* lots are in *my* hands." While acknowledging his limits as a creature, this man simultaneously refuses to have them removed; he remains on the level of immanence and, in this case, in the isolation typical of immanence. Instead of confiding his destiny into the hands of Another (we shall see that this constitutes the essence of hope), he keeps his destiny in his own hands, while declaring that he cannot preserve it.

Pride locks some men into their despair

According to Kierkegaard, there is still another form of despair, which constitutes in some way the very climax of despair. This

---

[7] Ps. 30:16. (RSV= Ps. 31:15).

latter type is fully conscious in a double sense: a man is conscious of his own despair and also conscious that there is a cure for *him*, that he could be helped out of his despair. In spite of all this, he settles for his despair, preferring, as it were, to be desperate rather than to be helped by another. (Augustine says "unhappy is the man who is too proud, too proud to accept mercy.")

This latter case is in complete defiance of reason. Can one imagine anything more irrational than the case of a man who endures the bitterest torments of despair, and yet prefers this pitiable state to extending his hand to another, begging for help? Here we touch upon one of the most mysterious depths of the human person, who, while granted the gift of reason, can be brought to hate reason. This is, according to Plato, the greatest evil which can befall man. This most mysterious factor in man is the one of his liberty, a liberty so abysmal that it *alone* can choose its own doom.

Freedom is now erroneously identified with arbitrariness

It may be in order at this point to investigate the genesis of human freedom. An unborn child constitutes a harmonious whole with its mother; but simultaneously, this preestablished harmony, being imposed, cannot lay claim to possessing the merits of a *union*. This harmony is rather a symbolic promise. This stage is followed by the one of birth in which the child, so to speak, conquers his character of full individuality; that is, he reaches a new decisive stage in his character as an individual person, fully capable of existing on his own. Yet, his development as a person is still so inadequate that a child lets himself be handled by his mother as if he were a thing; she takes him, cares for him, pampers him at will. This passivity leads people to consider a child as a toy, as a doll with which one can play.

But as the child grows and develops further, he is slowly led to an amazing discovery: he can say "no" to his mother's wishes; he can make up his own mind; he becomes conscious of the amazing, insuperable power of human liberty.

This discovery is symbolized by an attitude which all of us have had the chance of observing many times: a child called by his mother looks at her, seems to hesitate for a moment, and then runs as fast as his legs will carry him — in another direction! He is now enjoying the power of independence, and enjoying it so thoroughly that his satisfaction will immediately change into an outspoken rage the very moment that, caught by his mother, he is forced to give up his own plans for independent motion.

This craving for independence, for an ever clearer distinction between his wishes and the wishes of others, will keep increasing in the child throughout his development.

It will reach its climax at the time of puberty, the age characterized by a fierce stressing of one's independence, a general revolt against all laws and obligations, and a constant suspicion that one's sovereignty might be infringed upon.

This *defensive* attitude is so strongly outlined that "no" becomes symbolic of authentic freedom. Freedom is seen primarily as a powerful rejection of outward pressures and influences, as an assertion of the self against all other selves and against the world itself.

The weakness and impotence of this stage of development is evidenced by the fact that an educator conscious of this attitude in his pupil can easily bring him to do what he wishes him to do simply by carefully concealing his wish to have something done.

Subjectively speaking, the adolescent is drunk with his own independence, and totally overlooks the fact that he remains a slave; for his attitudes are dictated by reactions, by rejections which have a determining power over him. I remember that when my brother was fourteen or so, his main preoccupation was to persuade *me* of this complete and total independence (it is in any case an interesting fact that one tries to persuade others), while at the same time he remained a complete prey to the judgments of others. It was enough to tell him "I am sure you do not dare to do so or so" in order to bring him to do it, or try to do it, on the spot.

There is no doubt that many men remain forever in this imperfect stage of development. They make the grievous mistake of identifying true freedom with independence in the sense of negation and rejection.

This grants to the glorious human possibility of free choice a tragic character of irrational arbitrariness, the nature of which finds its most perfect and most pathetic expression in the philosophy of Jean Paul Sartre.

The phenomenon we have just described seems to set at odds two central human faculties: namely, rationality and liberty. Much of contemporary philosophy has settled for this antagonistic polarity, which is viewed as a hopeless dilemma. The philosophical result is what has been aptly called in contemporary terms *the irrational man*, the man swayed by unconscious drives and needs, the man who sees reason as a curse, and glories in his having freed himself from its demands.

This trend has taken root so powerfully in the twentieth century that it has conquered the domain of art. The latter no longer feels it desirable to follow an objective *logos*, to collaborate with forms pre-given in nature, but rather views these forms as illegitimate demands made upon the independent arbitrariness of its own creativity.

A closer analysis would take us too far from our present topic; but it is important to recall that true freedom and total arbitrariness have been wedded in the minds of many a contemporary thinker.

Freedom is meant to liberate us from selfishness

How luminous and refreshing is the thought of St. Augustine on the same topic. While fully acknowledging man's power of choice, while fully recognizing freedom to be a mark of the person's royal independence, a sign of his own matchless dignity, he nevertheless refuses to see in it the arbitrary rejection of any law. In his work *On Free Will*, St. Augustine makes it luminously clear that we should distinguish between the power to make a free decision (a power granted to all men) and the proper exercise of that power. Instead of viewing freedom as a means of self-centered defense against the world and its demands, he views it as an efficient means of liberation from the illegitimate demands of one's own selfishness. To be free, for St. Augustine, is infinitely more than to possess independence to do as one pleases; it is, above all, a liberation from the chain of pride and concupiscence enslaving me, which enables me to do what I know is good and right. To put it in few words: "I must liberate myself *from* my ties in order to be free *for* the demands of the world of values, and ultimately of God himself."

Freedom is the path to union with others

This detour on the topic of human freedom brings us back to our central theme: if man is to live as a person in the deep and true sense of this term, he must transcend the stage of development in which he views himself as a closed monad whose central task is to live on the alert out of fear that other monads might infringe upon his autocratic sovereignty. He will rather understand that — to quote Gabriel Marcel — "to be a person is to be with."

Man is not an isolated monad; he is born into a universe structured according to moral laws which are given *a priori* and

The Art of Living

which shed a luminous meaning on a world that would be meaningless without them.

These laws are not invented by man and cannot be of his own making. Rather they invite him to assent, not in a state of lazy passivity, but with the fervor of a glorious collaboration which, far from being unfree, is in fact the very peak of freedom. This collaboration includes both freedom over himself and a free response to something above him, a testimony to his transcendence.

Our deepest relations with human creatures admirably confirm the nature of true freedom. In love and in marriage, we find both the victory over one's selfishness, one's immanence, and simultaneously the meeting of two liberties united in one love. It is deeply meaningful that throughout the history of the Church, marriage has been used as a font of analogies. Whereas Sartre sees the sexual union as a brutal conquest of another's body, as an impotent effort to conquer his freedom, love is in fact a gloriously free giving of oneself to another and a grateful acceptance of his own gift to me.

We now see that the deepest dimension of human freedom is not found in autocratic and independent decisions, as the adolescent tends to believe, but rather is a concerting with the symphony of values pervading the universe. To enter into dialogue with another, to grasp his innermost structure, to respond to the demands of the world of values — far from limiting man's freedom — is possible only in and through a transcendently free act, which can spring only from the deepest part of a person's soul.

After this rather long detour, we can understand why the man who prefers his own despair to being helped out of it, far from being free in the deepest sense of this term, is actually imprisoned in the cramp of an ego that has become a caricature of an *imago Dei*. Shrunken in itself, turning ceaselessly upon itself, it is like a man in prison who, instead of trying to liberate himself, willingly binds and gags himself.

Optimism is a disposition rather than a response

To see that hope is necessarily linked to man's transcendence and is possible only if man breaks through the circle of his limits, we must first clearly separate hope from superficially similar phenomena. The most obvious of these is *optimism*. Because of the misleading looseness of our use of words, we are often tempted to say that an optimistic person is full of hope; he is never cast down; and he keeps looking forward to a carefree and enjoyable future.

But this attitude has nothing to do with hope, for in optimism we are facing a purely dispositional trait, a purely immanent tendency which is totally deprived of the character of a response. The optimistic person will be so without any objective motivation; he is neither responding to favorable circumstances nor to a transcendent factor that can waive threatening facts.

Optimism is essentially a sort of inner dynamism, a propelling force which keeps one going. But optimism is simultaneously coupled with a sort of blindness, for the optimistic person does not see the objective character of a situation and then respond with optimism, but he is optimistic on principle, and this very disposition precisely blinds him to the objective character of a situation.

Optimism is so much rooted in immanence that it is quite possible to imagine a person characterized by an innate optimism suddenly falling into the dark pit of despair the very moment that his supply of optimism is exhausted. Optimism can be compared to a fuel, and the very moment a person runs out of this fuel, his optimism comes to a sudden and unforeseen halt.

Wishful thinking is not hope

We must also avoid confusing hope with wishful thinking — a confusion all the more likely to occur since these two experiences seem alike. Obviously, people will tell you, to hope that your friend will recover from his illness is equivalent to believing that he will do so because you wish it, and this wishing gains so much impetus that you are led to an inner conviction that it will be so.

Let us grant that every act of hope shares with wishful thinking the feature of carrying within itself a wish (that is, if I hope for something, I necessarily wish its realization). Let us grant further that both wishful thinking and hoping are characterized by an inner conviction that something will come to pass or that some menace will be averted. Nonetheless, these similarities should not blind us to the essential differences between the two types of experience.

In wishful thinking, the very dynamism of my desire blinds me to the reality of certain facts. I actually do not see them because I refuse to do so, or I imagine something to exist because I wish it to be. In hope, on the contrary, I seem to be granted a peculiar clarity of vision as to the drama of the situation. I have no illusion. I see with pitiless clarity that, humanly speaking, a situation is desperate. I experience all the anguish inherent in this despair, but I rely on a transcendent factor and thus *refuse to see tragedy as the last word*. I break through the circle of immanent causalities, and transcend to a sphere in which the pitiless unfolding of immanent laws ceases to hold sway.

Hope is grounded in God

We now come to the decisive factor: metaphysically speaking, every act of hoping is grounded in God. Gabriel Marcel has shown with remarkable clarity that the very essence of hope rests on a *hope in*. When I tremble for the life of a beloved person, I transcend not only myself but the whole earthly reality and turn to God, the infinitely merciful and mighty.

I trust that the welfare of this loved one is not my own exclusive concern, but that God Himself cares for him, loves him even more than I love him.

As a matter of fact, in such moments I experience my love as a partaking of God's infinite love. In spite of the desperate darkness which surrounds me, I refuse to let myself be enclosed in it; I refuse to interpret it as the last ultimate reality.

The very fact that the situation I find myself in is truly desperate, the fact that I must *hope against hope*, far from making it an irrational act, forces me to transcend the rational sphere and to trust the blinding light of a suprarational reality in which my hope is grounded.

This should make it clear that every act of hope is primarily a response to God, to His infinite goodness, to His almightiness, and to the fact that God loves us infinitely. Every true *hope that* something will come to pass presupposes a *hope in*, whether or not the hoping person realizes it.

A theoretical atheist who, when threatened by despair about the grave illness of his beloved wife, refuses to let himself be engulfed in this darkness and even proclaims that he still *hopes* that she will recover, is making an implicit appeal to the goodness of God. For every *hope that* essentially presupposes a *hope in* Someone, whose goodness is the guarantee that my *hope that* will not be in vain.

The point is that a believer consciously grounds his hope in God and, trusting in God's absolute goodness, hopes that the last word of human existence is joy. This is admirably expressed in the words of the Psalmist: "In Thee, O Lord, I have hoped (*hope in*); let me never be put to confusion (*hope that*)."[8]

[8] Ps. 70:1. (RSV= Ps. 71:1).

A theoretical atheist, on the contrary, consciously *hopes that* an event will occur despite contrary human prognoses; but he fails to realize that in such moments he has become a practical believer. For in such moments he believes implicitly in the goodness of an infinitely powerful Being who can avert an evil or cancel a threat.

It is no easy matter to be a consistent atheist! A military leader said that he never met an atheist on the battlefield. My personal experiences led me to a similar conclusion: many a person calls himself an atheist, while he is in fact rejecting an abominable caricature of God imposed upon him by a disastrous religious education. Others, while calling themselves atheists, fail to diagnose properly their attitude toward God; they expect faith to be a rational conviction based on knowledge, and thus fail to realize that faith, like a precious seed, has already blossomed in their souls.

Men hope in God explicitly or implicitly

We must thus distinguish between two very different types of hope. In the first type of hope — the more authentic one — the basis of all *hoping that* is the *hoping in* consciously grounded in God. There is a conscious response to the omnipotence and goodness of God, out of which our *hoping that* springs.

Our earthly situation is oftentimes such that God seems to be unconcerned about terrestrial affairs. How often does the Psalmist exclaim "Arise, why sleepest Thou, O Lord?"[9] But in hope, I trust that in spite of all appearances to the contrary, God in His infinite goodness cares for His creatures — nay more, He wants their happiness.

[9] Ps. 43:23. (RSV= Ps. 44:23).

Then there is the case of a man who does not believe in God. But let us suppose that someone he loves is threatened by a terrible disease and, in spite of the desperate character of the situation, he tells us that he hopes against hope. Consciously, he only *hopes that* this beloved person will recover, but deep down he presupposes in some way that over and above the complex set of natural causes there is a factor, a something, a Someone, that can avert the danger.

Death can provoke despair in those aware of life's goodness

The great threat menacing human existence is the threat of despair. As soon as one starts meditating on the nature of temporal and finite existence, one understands that it leads to a blind alley whose end is despair.

Yet the threat of despair is as little related to pessimism as hope is related to optimism. Kierkegaard's stand on despair remains true even if one rejected his pessimism concerning natural goods. In reality life is rich in blissful experiences and offers us high goods with great values which can and do delight us. We should not forget the words of the *Sanctus:* "Heaven and earth are full of your glory." Buddhist pessimism, which equates existence with suffering, is in no way warranted by authentic reality. This earth is not exclusively a valley of tears; it is also resonant with innumerable messages of God in all true and great values. What gifts are granted to us in beauty; what a blessing is the gift of true love, of a happy marriage, of a deep friendship; what delight can one find in the seeking of truth and in its contemplation once found.

No, the man whose vision is undistorted sees not only suffering and evil; he is also aware of innumerable and glorious goods which objectively sing God's praise. And yet the menace of despair remains, because the more beautiful life is, the greater is the horror of death, the more unbearable is the knowledge that we seem condemned to return to nothingness. For a radical pessimist such as Leopardi, death is rather a relief; for the Buddhist, the cessation of individual existence is an ideal. But death is precisely a source of despair for the one who sees all the glorious goods which are bestowed upon us in life.

Historical time can be a reason for despair

The words "it is passed," "it is all over," "it is no more" are typical of our earthly existence and are simultaneously loaded with despair. Which one of us has not tasted the bitterness of going back to a place where we once experienced something deep or beautiful, only to learn that this will never, never come back; it has passed.

It is not by accident that so many religions have interpreted time as a cyclical recurrence, thereby avoiding carefully the "never again." It is probable that the theory of reincarnation, so widespread in many religions, testifies to the same fact: man's longing to escape from the pitiless flow of time.

Historians of religion agree that one of the most revolutionary conceptions transmitted by the Bible is that of historical time, which implies an irreversible movement forward. It is simultaneously of essential importance to understand that *at the very moment* when the possibility of despairing is revealed to man in all its horror, the light of hope is diffused in the human heart through reference to a transhistorical, eternal promise.

Through a process of religious desacralization, Western man, while keeping the historical interpretation of time, has often rejected the possible redemption of time through eternity. He has thereby opened the door wide to despair, a despair which lurks today in all of modern life despite the futile attempt to replace the historical perspective leading to eternity by an immanent progress supposedly leading to a terrestrial paradise. Whether we think of Heidegger's philosophy, of his fascination with death as the truth of man's existence, or whether we think of Sartre's delight in the absurdity of the world, we find ourselves in a land of *No Exit* (the title of Sartre's play), a land of despair. "Too late," "it is not worth the game," "it will soon be over anyway," and so forth are words of despair.

In Sartre, Hell is no longer interpreted as a transhistorical eternal punishment, but is "incarnated" in the present life, at the present moment. For him, Hell is other people.

Hope is a response to God as loving creator

In authentic hope, on the contrary, we find a radical nonacceptance of an evil as final, as the last word, but this rejection has nothing to do with a revolt. For in revolt, my rejection is impotent. I knock my head against a wall. In hope, on the contrary, while seeing that, humanly speaking, a situation is doomed, I refuse to "close" time, to "petrify" the situation, to "freeze" it in its tragedy.

In hope, I always transcend the framework of earthly finitude. I liberate myself from the phenomenon of "it is all over" and trust that this darkness will be changed into light, that this death is a passage toward resurrection. In fact, hope is a response to God as loving Creator; in hope I trust the creative power of God who can "make all things new."[10]

Hope requires our collaboration with it

We should now turn to the decisive question: whether we are free to hope or not. But the question "Can I give hope to myself?"

[10]Rev. 21:5.

cannot be severed from another, namely, "Is there a *reason* for men to hope?" It would be absurd indeed to endorse Sartre's metaphysical outlook and then declare cheerfully "but obviously, we are full of hope."

Hope is essentially a response, and consequently presupposes an awareness of a reality capable of eliciting this response.

Gabriel Marcel rightly remarks that the more something is personally related to myself, the less it is in my power to conquer it. Happiness, faith, hope, love, and peace, which are existentially related to the very core of man's being, are not under man's control, but call for a dialogical collaboration.

One of the striking weaknesses of Stoicism (and of Buddhism for that matter) is its claim that one can reach an inner state of contentment and equanimity quite independently of the objective situation, and of whether this inner contentment is warranted or not.

As Heidegger chooses to ignore God, he is perfectly consistent in describing human life as being woven by threads of anguish and anxiety. Rationally speaking, despair is the only adequate answer to a world without God. In a striking passage in his *Being and Time*, Heidegger claims that man's arch experience is this "unshelteredness," his being thrown into the world, his metaphysical insecurity.

The question is whether Heidegger does not typify the third type of individual described by Kierkegaard, the one who prefers his own despair to being helped out of it.

Quite clearly, I cannot give hope to myself, just as I cannot give faith or love to myself. But far from ending at this point, the question truly begins here.

To say "either I can give hope to myself by a sheer act of will, or there is nothing that I can do about it, nothing at all," is to create a false alternative. As many people are prone to identify hope with an innate optimism, they justify their own despair by saying: "My nature has always been inclined to discouragement. I am made so; I cannot help it."

If, as Marcel has pointed out, hope is a *hope in* someone, the whole question takes a remarkably different nature: a relationship must be established between myself and this someone, a communion that will be my guarantee of salvation the very moment that I am menaced by despair.

Marcel remarks that in hope, there is a prophetic note: "This will be, or that will not be." But this should not make us overlook the fact that hope as well as faith has a heroic element, because if we limit our outlook to what is visible and see death as the terminus of human existence, despair *is* the only rational answer.

Although a reason for hope is given to us in Christian Revelation, nevertheless our collaboration is fully required, and this fact clearly distinguishes the response of hope from any expectation based on natural knowledge, whereby we feel the firm ground of everyday reality under our feet. This heroic element applies primarily to *hope in;* yet there is still a paradoxical feature in *hope that*.

While hope is related to things which are beyond my power, that I can in no way command, it nevertheless requires my utmost collaboration. The fact that the end result is beyond my reach should in no way encourage me to adopt an attitude of passive numbness.

On the contrary, I should do with utmost care whatever I can do, knowing that my humble efforts cannot lay any claim to a victory if God does not intervene, but trusting that my loving collaboration has its *meaning* quite independently of its efficacy.

From this point of view, it should be clear that hope is at the extreme pole of fatalism which says "whatever will be, will be; what can I do about it?"

Love makes hope easier

We see that hope presupposes God's existence, but grant that atheists can hope, due to the fact that deep down they have some awareness of God. Hope unveils their objective metaphysical link with God. As Father de Lubac put it strikingly in his work on the knowledge of God, what we need to do to bring a man to believing in God is not to pile up arguments, but much rather to remove a crust of prejudices and intellectual dirt that has covered up man's metaphysical bond with his Creator.

When the deepest human experiences are threatened (for example, when the life of a beloved person is in danger), human beings are often led to discover their capacity to hope. It is as if the intensity of love helped one to remove a crust of self-centered indifference which prevents men from realizing that hope is the foundation of our human existence.

This capacity to hope is the fundamental gesture of man when he is conscious of his creaturehood, and this is especially the case in loving. The true lover, shaken out of all mediocre security, experiences his creaturehood and, through it, turns to the Creator.

Christian hope is based on firm ground

Our hope as *Christians* — although requiring, as we saw, our free collaboration, although possessing a heroic element and the character of a leap — is based on a firm ground. It is objectively *due* as a response to the ultimate reality disclosed to us in Revelation. It is no longer a blind hope, but flows organically from our faith.

Our *hope that* is grounded in our *hope in*, in the God who lives and sees, as St. Augustine puts it, the God who has revealed Himself in Christ. Free from all illusions, fully conscious of the tragedy of death, the true Christian keeps his eyes fixed on the ultimate, supernatural reality, which gives to all the universe its true meaning.

St. Paul says: "I know in whom I believe."[11] We can add: "I know in whom I hope." We hope in Christ in whom, as the Preface of the *Mass for the Dead* says, "has dawned for us the hope of a blessed resurrection, heartening with a promise of immortality to come those of us who are saddened by the certainty of dying."

[11] 2 Tim. 1:12.

8

Gratitude

Gratitude can be given to God or it can be directed to other human persons. In this final chapter, we shall consider in detail the role that each of these two "kinds" of gratitude should play in our lives.[12]

Gratitude to God

Gratitude to God is one of the fundamental, basic characteristics of the religious life. The words "Who are you and who am I?" found in St. Francis's prayer reveal the basic confrontation of the creature, mere "dust and ashes,"[13] with the unattainable, absolute majesty of God revealed in the sacred humanity of Christ: "The mystery of the Incarnation illuminates to our spiritual eyes the new light of your splendor in such a way that while we perceive

---

[12] This chapter first appeared posthumously as a booklet entitled *Über die Dankbarkeit* (1980: EOS Verlag Erzabtei St. Ottilien).

[13] Gen. 18:27.

God with our eyes, He may enkindle in us the love of invisible blessings."[14]

Gratitude for our existence as a person is also a part of our fundamental bearing toward God, as is gratitude for all the natural goods and, above all, for His great wonders (*magnalia Dei*), for His graces, and for His infinite mercy. Thus prayers of gratitude should be the centerpiece of the life of prayer.

Balduin Schwarz had profound insights on the matter of gratitude to God.[15] Specifically, he showed how giving thanks in response to a favorable outcome of events or for that happiness which is not due to other people's actions, can only mean thanking God, which implicitly presupposes the existence of a good God and His Providence. Like hope, the affective response of gratitude implies a tacit reliance on the existence of a benevolent and all-powerful God, even by those who have not yet found Him.

Gratitude is a basic response to God, profoundly connected with ultimate subordination to Him — the absolute Lord — and with adoring love for Him, the infinitely holy one, the quintessence of all beauty and majesty. However, gratitude itself is something *sui generis*, reducible to nothing else, an ultimate, irreplaceable *word* in the relation of man to God.

Gratitude presupposes apprehension of values

Included in this primary *word* of man to God is apprehension and full understanding of the values which inhere in beneficial

---

[14]"*Per incarnati Verbi mysterium nova mentis nostrae oculis lux tuae claritatis infulsit: ut dum visibiliter Deum cognoscimus, per hunc in invisibilium amorem rapiamur*" (Preface of Christmas).

[15]"Über die Dankbarkeit" in Balduin Schwarz, *Wirklichkeit der Mitte, Beiträge zu einer Strukturanthropologie: Festgabe für August Vetter* (Freiburg und München: Karl Alber, 1968), 679-704.

goods for us, with which God's love continually overwhelms us. Values constitute the true dynamism of being, which does not at all contradict the inherent greatness of being. All the enthusiasm for the "dynamic" that is found in Hegel and Heidegger, the idolizing of motion as opposed to "static" being, completely misses the true dynamic that is present in value-filled being as opposed to naked and indifferent being.

In several of our works we have previously pointed out the fundamental importance of the full apprehension of values.[16] The breadth, the spiritual stature, and the richness of a person's spirit actually depends on his grasp of values. The fundamental ontological importance of values, of the being that is the bearer of a value, of the valuable as opposed to the indifferent, becomes apparent if we consider what is meant by grasping values in contrast to being value-blind. We have a premonition of what the fiery being of values — this highest dimension of being — means; we sense that we have brushed against a primary mystery.[17]

---

[16] What would the world be if there were only the distinction between the means and the end, and nothing to raise these concepts above their gray neutrality? In that case, an answer about the ultimate meaning and the *raison d'être* of the universe would only be possible if the whole world could be shown to be a network of final causality. For the importance of *the end* compared with *the means* does not reveal the true *raison d'être* of the end. What is more, while the *raison d'être* of an existing being as a means to an end only has the character of something indispensable and essential for the end, the very reason for its existence depends on the importance of the end. And if the true *raison d'être* of the end is not clear to us, then all that which is grounded only in indispensability also remains without a true *raison d'être*.

[17] The abyss of nothingness awakens in us the *horror vacui* (the terror of the void) as soon as we pretend that objective being is totally neutral and indifferent and that every value is only a subjective illusion. The inconceivable barrenness, the absurdity and nothingness of a world in which there is no objective value and disvalue, can hardly be imagined. We venture to assert that the legion of those who attempt to deny the existence

The Art of Living

The vital importance of the capacity to apprehend values becomes clear in light of the fact that value is the core of being. A person incapable of grasping values and understanding them as values is no real person. Without the grasp of values, the core of the dialogue between subject and object becomes impossible and the full transcendence of knowledge becomes nonexistent. If the capacity for apprehending objective values were to be taken from man, he would be cut off from the innermost life of the cosmos and especially from God. St Augustine's words "You have made us for Yourself"[18] would no longer have validity.

Gratitude is a specific response to beneficial goods

Gratitude toward God presupposes the perception and understanding of the values of all of God's gifts, but it also presupposes the perception and understanding of the nature of beneficial goods for the person.[19] Gratitude is a specific response to beneficial goods for the person.[20]

For example, in gratitude for the gift of knowledge, I must grasp not only the value of knowledge itself, but also the gift that

of objective values — the relativists, immanentists, and subjectivists — can never existentially and consistently conceive of an entirely indifferent world, a world that is filled with the icy breath of absolute neutrality and indifference. They can no more do this than the gainsayers of an absolute truth can consistently construct a world without something existing objectively — without, that is, absolute truth.

[18] St. Augustine, *Confessions*, Bk. 1, Ch. 1.

[19] I have spoken in detail concerning beneficial goods in other places. See Dietrich von Hildebrand, *Ethics* (Chicago: Franciscan Herald Press, 1953), Ch. 5, "The Primacy of Value," 72-74, and Ch. 7, "The Categories of Importance as Properties of Being," 79-94 .

[20] Cf. Dietrich von Hildebrand, *Gesammelte Werke*, vol. 9, *Moralia*, Ch. 5 (Regensburg: Habbel, 1980), 105-116.

knowledge represents *for me*. With this gift I grasp the *pro*, the gesture of the gift *qua* gift which is friendly and affirming for me. The comprehension of this *pro* is inextricably linked with the personal God, with His goodness and love which are personally directed at me.

Gratitude is intimately related to God

Thus we are touched by a blissful, intimate dimension of the religious life, the awareness of the primary source of all happiness, which is that we are loved by God. Gratitude is a specific response to God's love manifested to us by His wonderful gifts. Gratitude includes our understanding, first of all, of the value of this good; second, of the objective good for me inherent in this gift; third, of the goodness of God in its inconceivably sacred beauty; and finally, that the goodness is intended for me, that His love touches me personally. We can then surmise what a central factor gratitude is in our relationship with God and what a high value it bears as a response to all these great gifts.

In genuine gratitude toward God man becomes beautiful. He emerges from immanence, from the confines of ego-relatedness and enters into the blissful giving of himself to God, the quintessence of all glory, into the realm of goodness and true kindness. In gratitude, man becomes great and expansive. Blessed and victorious freedom blooms in his soul.

Gratitude is also deeply linked to humility. The thankful person is conscious of the fact that he is a beggar before God and possesses no right in relation to God on which he can insist, that all is a gift of the goodness of God and that he can make no claim against God.

Kierkegaard speaks wonderfully about gratitude and its intimate relation to God:

And now that I must talk about my God-relationship —
about what every day is repeated in my prayer of thanksgiving for the indescribable things He has done for me, so
infinitely much more than ever I could have expected — I
must speak about the experience which has taught me to be
amazed, amazed at God, at His love and at what a man's
impotence is capable of with His aid, about what has taught
me to long for eternity and not to fear that I might find it
tiresome, since it is exactly the situation I need so as to have
nothing else to do but to give thanks.[21]

The person who is filled with gratitude toward God, whose life
is permeated by this primary attitude of gratitude, is also the only
person who is truly awake. He is the opposite of the apathetic,
obtuse person, who remains in that state of half-wakefulness
which suffices for the fulfillment of life's practical necessities. He
is the opposite of the person who remains on the periphery and
takes everything for granted.

Here there is a decided analogy to the sphere of knowledge.
Homo sapiens differs from *homo faber* not only because he does not
take the reality around him for granted, investigating it only for
pragmatic reasons, but is full of astonishment, awake to the question of the essence and meaning of things, and possesses an
understanding of values. (Both Plato and Aristotle refer to *wonder*
as the beginning of all philosophy.)

Something analogous to this awakening, this emerging from a
solely pragmatic outlook, occurs in the man whose life is permeated by true gratitude to God. He is awakened from the apathy and
superficiality of taking things for granted to astonishment at the

---

[21] Sören Kierkegaard, *The Point of View for My Work as an Author*, trans.
Walter Lowrie (New York: Harper Torchbooks, 1962), 66-67.

gifts of God and the inexhaustibly blissful mystery of the infinite love and mercy of God.

The feeling of gratitude urges the person toward expression in an act of thanksgiving. There is a general tendency in man to give expression to what fills his heart. "For out of the abundance of the heart, the mouth speaks," says Christ.[22] However, this general tendency is actualized in very different ways.

Acts of expression differ from declarations and social acts

For example, in our *Metaphysics of Community*, we described the difference between a pure, spontaneous expression of that which fills our heart and a meaningful, intentional declaration of love.[23]

The tendency which urges us to give expression to what intensely fills our heart becomes most apparent in those social acts in which this manifestation essentially belongs to the accomplishment of the inner act, to its interpersonal character. Different from such acts of expression are social acts such as promising, informing, questioning, and judging.

But when it is not a question of such social acts, the urge for expression stands out clearly. This expression is more dynamic than intentional, but it belongs to man's very nature. The deep link between body and soul reveals itself in this act. Expression typically involves the body, whether it be in *words* like "I gladly carved it on the bark of every tree"[24] or in *singing* ("Singing is the

[22] Luke 6:45.

[23] Dietrich von Hildebrand, *Metaphysik der Gemeinschaft* in *Gesammelte Werke*, vol. 4, ch. 2 (Regensburg: Habbel, 1975), 21-30.

[24] "*Ich* schnitt' es gern in alle Rinden ein" in Franz Schubert, *Die schöne Müllerin*, Op. 25, 7. "Ungeduld" in Wilhelm Mueller's song series.

act of lovers"),[25] whether in laughing, weeping, kneeling, or standing. This pure form of expression is clearly different from meaningfully intentional declarations (such as, for example, of love). For such a declaration not only has an interpersonal function, but is a unique, meaningful intention to send the beam of love into the consciousness of the beloved, an important step in the process of union with him, a fulfillment of love's intention of union (*intentio unionis*).

But such an intentional declaration can also, and at the same time be an *expression*, without the essential distinction of the two categories being compromised. On the one hand, the act of thanking is first of all a *declaration* of gratitude. Like the declaration of love, it can only be rendered in relation to the one to whom it is directed, in relation to the one to whom one feels gratitude. On the other hand, thanking also has the character of a *social act*; for it is not only the declaration of our attitude of gratitude to which we give expression, but it is also directed toward the gift for which I give thanks. In this respect, thanking resembles promising or informing. Not only does another person constitute the theme (in that he is the partner whom I address), but the gift for which I give thanks is also part of that theme.

Finally, there is in thanking also the expression of an *overflowing affectivity*, which St. Augustine refers to when he says that to sing is typical of the lover.

Expression of gratitude brings about wholeness

There is a new solemnity when the spoken word is transformed into song. This sublime, totally unpragmatic note originates in the

---

[25]"*Cantare autem . . . negotium esse solet amantium.*" St. Augustine, *Sermon* 33.1.

longing to give expression to our feelings. It comes not only from
the aforementioned dynamic character of expression; it springs as
well from that wholeness which is achieved when something is
meaningfully completed. This wholeness is missing when deeply-
rooted spiritual attitudes and value-responses go unexpressed, but
it is achieved when they are revealed by being expressed through
the body.

It is no accident that prayers of gratitude occupy such an
important place in the Liturgy. Let us only consider the three
unique hymns: the *Benedictus*, the *Magnificat* and the *Nunc
Dimittis*, which celebrate the transition from the Old to the New
Testament. The reverently expectant, hopeful attitude of the Old
Testament merges into the overflowing, grateful attitude of the
New. Indeed, both attitudes are united in a unique way. When St.
Augustine says at the end of *The City of God*, "There we shall
have leisure and we shall see; we shall see and we shall love; we
shall love and we shall praise,"[26] the word *praise* — together with
the statement "we shall praise" — refers to that dimension of
expression which belongs to the consummation, to that "which
will be in the end without end."[27]

Even in eternity, in which there will be only a transfigured
reality, praise (and with it and in it also the explicit giving of
thanks) retains its full importance.

Gratitude yearns for expression in thanksgiving

Can we imagine a person whose heart is overflowing with
gratitude toward God but who never feels compelled to give it

[26] St Augustine, *The City of God*, Bk. 22, Ch. 30: "*Ibi vacabimus, et
videbimus; videbimus, et amabimus; amabimus, et laudabimus.*"
[27] Ibid.

expression in his own prayer of gratitude? Of course not! Such a lack of an inner impulse to thank God in spoken prayer for the reception of His gifts and graces would be a clear indication that gratitude toward God does not yet occupy the rightful place in his heart. The above-mentioned hymns express the overflowing gratitude for the receiving of a great and fateful gift: Zacharias gives thanks for the miracle of the birth of John the Baptist; the Most Blessed Virgin for the incomprehensible, unique grace of being selected as the Virgin mother of the Redeemer; Simeon for the grace of being allowed before his death to see and to hold the promised Redeemer in his arms. How essential, how crucial for true gratitude is this explicit act of thanking, this prayer of thanksgiving expressed in words.

We shall return to this connection between genuine gratitude and the specific act of thanksgiving in still more detail when we analyze gratitude to human persons. But at this time we need to bring out several other aspects of gratitude to God.

Profound happiness comes to the truly grateful person

First of all, we want to discuss the profound relationship between true happiness and gratitude. Certainly, acknowledging the values on which gratitude is based is a primary source of happiness. Above all, the consciousness of God's love and mercy toward us, which is, indeed, included in our understanding of a gift of God and of its character as a beneficial good for us, is plainly the primary source of all true, imperishable happiness.

But we should also stress the happiness that is inherent in feeling grateful and in the resulting act of gratitude. This is the happiness of inner freedom and of the humility inherently linked to it which belongs to the thankful person. We only need to distinguish clearly between the man who takes for granted his existence as a person, the gifts that God has bestowed on him, as well as the love and friendship of others which have been given to him, and the man who takes nothing for granted, but who acknowledges that everything is an unmerited gift. The latter stands within the truth, while the former is blindly imprisoned in his obtuse indifference. Clearly desolation marks the life of the person who neither understands the abundance and value of the gifts he has received, nor knows that they are unmerited gifts, nor recognizes that in them shines the goodness, mercy, and love of God! This comparison illustrates the profound happiness that can only be known by the thankful person.

Each person receives a range of beneficial goods

A many-tiered hierarchy is to be found within the beneficial goods for us, both with regard to their inherent value as well as with regard to the role that they play in our life. Thus God's gift of an extraordinary talent (whether it be intellectual or artistic, creative or reproductive) has a continuous importance which resonates through our whole life, in contradistinction to, for example, the gift of a single beautiful journey. Even more fundamental gifts from God include our capacity for the knowledge of values, our potential to love, and even our free will; these are greater gifts than even the precious gift of a great friendship. Oddly enough, we become all the less aware that a beneficial good for us is a gift from God the more fundamental and formal it is. We are more easily filled with gratitude toward God for the loving union with another person than for our existence as a person, although the latter is the primary presupposition for everything else, for all happiness and for eternal bliss.

How many of us are conscious of our existence as an inconceivable gift? How many of us take this fundamental gift for granted?

The Art of Living

Hand in hand with our transformation in Christ goes a continuous growing awareness of God's gifts, both the appreciation of their value and the recognition of their formal importance. Possessing any beneficial good becomes less a matter of course. Everything is ever more seen to be an unmerited gift; everything is perceived as a reason for unlimited gratitude toward God and the urge to thank Him expressly for everything becomes stronger and stronger.

Goods and evils call, respectively, for a different response

Of course, man's life is not only filled with the gifts of God, but also contains objective evils for him, crosses of every kind. In this respect, there are great differences in people's lives. Often there is a richly blessed life right next to a ruined life or one burdened with suffering such as deformities or illnesses. Furthermore, we must remember not only that there is a distinction between a happy life and a life full of suffering, but also that every life contains both great gifts on the one hand and hard suffering and crosses to bear on the other.[28]

In contrast to the unfathomable gift of personal existence and of life on earth stands the terrible cross of death. Hand in hand with the great gift of unity with the beloved goes worry about his life, the fear of separation through death, indeed, even the possibility that he could cease requiting our love. Although we sing "heaven and earth are full of Your glory," the life of man, in spite of all the gifts of God, is a *vallis lacrimarum*, a vale of tears.

Then the question arises: what kind of response to crosses and suffering does God require of us? Should our response to them

---

[28] When we examine whether something is a positive gift from God or a cross, we will restrict ourselves to the dispensations of God, and omit the consideration of sufferings that issue from our guilt and sinfulness.

likewise be one of gratitude, because we know that even the crosses and suffering are imposed or permitted by the infinite love of God?

It has been frequently asserted that he who truly loves Christ and is transformed in Him, gives thanks even for suffering and crosses because they represent a special communion with Christ — the bearing of the Cross with Him. Indeed, some say there should be no difference in our response of gratitude whether God bestows joy or imposes suffering.

Nonetheless, however true and profound may be the view that sees in suffering, in grateful resignation, and in self-sacrificing love imposed on us by God the gift of being allowed to share the Cross of Christ, it cannot be denied that there is a profound difference between gratitude for a great good and submissive, resigned acceptance of a great evil. The *Magnificat* of the most Blessed Virgin is obviously a different response than the attitude of the Mother of God standing at the Cross.

> At the Cross her station keeping,
> stood the mournful mother weeping,
> close to Jesus to the last.[29]

The essence of gratitude includes joy. The resigned acceptance of a cross in itself contains no joy. If it amounts to an heroic joy in the sense of gratitude at being allowed to share the Cross of Christ, this does not change the fact that the joy inherent in gratitude is intimately linked to the positive character of a gift.

---

[29] *Stabat mater dolorosa / Juxta crucem lacrimosa / Dum pependit filius.* From the *Stabat Mater* by Jacopone da Todi in the Sequence of the Mass of the Seven Sorrows of the Blessed Virgin Mary. English translation in the *Daily Missal of the Mystical Body*, ed. Maryknoll Fathers (New York: P.J. Kenedy and Sons, 1956), 1262.

The Art of Living

Sufferings exist for the sake of joy

In order to understand that the responses to a positive gift and to a cross should be different, we have to be conscious that happiness has priority over suffering. The mystery that the redemption of man occurred through Christ's passion and death on the Cross must not permit us to forget (as Father Heribert Holzapfel, O.F.M. noted) that sufferings are only there for the sake of joy.

The mystery of the unfathomable suffering of Christ, which constitutes a mysterious unfolding of the infinite love of the God-man Jesus Christ for God the Father and for mankind, must not cloak the fact that the redemption constitutes the way to sanctification of the individual person and to the resulting glorification of God, and also opens the gate to our eternal happiness. The greatness and depth of the passion of Christ causes us to pray in adoration:

> Wounded with His every wound,
> Steep my soul till it hath swooned
> In His very blood away.[30]

But this fact must not be allowed to obscure our knowledge that the passion of Christ is the way to eternal happiness for those redeemed and transformed in Christ. The sufferings of Christ, which move us to our very marrow, and His love, in which He pours out His blood for us, intoxicating our heart and causing us to pray "Blood of Christ, inebriate me,"[31] must not allow us to forget that the eternal goal is not participation in the Cross, but rather the blessed face-to-face vision of the God-man Jesus Christ

---

[30] Ibid., 1263: *Fac me plagis vulnerari / Fac me cruce inebriari / Et cruore Filii.*
[31] *"Sanguis Christi, inebria me"* from the medieval prayer *Anima Christi.*

116

reigning in transfigured glory in eternity. We pray for this face-to-face vision with the words:

> Beholding Your fair face revealed,
> Your glory shall I be blessed to see.[32]

Objective distinctions should not be blurred

There is a general danger for the deeply religious person of falling into a certain nihilism, which first seems to be the fruit of a special religious zeal but in reality, like every blurring of objective distinctions, has disastrous consequences. Instead of *nihilism* one could also say *uniformity*.

On the one hand, a disordered (or mistaken) desire for unity underlies this tendency — a need to ignore basic, outspoken differences in order to reduce everything to a common denominator. This urge has led to countless errors in philosophy. Some believe that discovery of an important fact means that the philosopher's stone has been found whereby everything can be explained. Others stretch analogies in different fields to such an extent that the essence of that field is seen in a false light or is even completely misunderstood in its very nature. This general tendency comes to the fore especially when a thinker aims at constructing a "system." We must avoid that temptation, especially in the religious realm.

The theologian Ockham, for example, believes that he enhances the absolute greatness and glory of God when he abolishes the decisive distinction between God's positive commandments and His moral commandments of God. In reality, by denying the

---

[32]"*Ut, te revelata cernens facie, / Visu sim beatus tuae gloriae.*" From St. Thomas Aquinas's hymn "*Adoro Te Devote.*" English translation by Robert Anderson and Johann Moser in *Devoutly I Adore Thee* (Manchester, NH: Sophia Institute Press, 1993), 71.

primary distinction of good and indifferent (or even of good and evil), the idea of God's nature is undermined, and the infinitely good, holy God is changed into an arbitrary, absolute lord; indeed, the most central and essential quality of God is denied. This is why we describe these attempts as *nihilism*.

Acceptance (not gratitude) is the right response to crosses

Nihilism also underlies the attempt, perceived as the highest heroism, to equate the response to a cross that has been imposed on us with the response to a great and wonderful gift of God. Some people say, for example,

> Everything is an emanation of the infinite love of God, the answering of which is the important thing. Therefore we must thank God in the same way for a cross imposed upon us as for a profoundly wonderful beneficial good for us. We ought to transcend the question of what makes us happy or of what deeply distresses us and press forward to the love of God. Does His love not manifest itself in both? Isn't the love of God for us, His merciful will to draw us to Himself and to prepare us for the eternal union with Him, the most important thing in all that is imposed on us by God?

Certainly! But it is precisely in this merciful love, which has called us to eternal blessedness, that the primacy of blessedness in comparison to all suffering is fully expressed. In approaching the merciful love of God we see clearly that the reality and the absolute distinction between bliss and sorrow is included in that love. Furthermore it is in accord with God's decrees for us to make a clear distinction between a beneficial gift and a cross. For although everything is an emanation of the infinite love of God — even the permitting of incomprehensible, terrible crosses such as the death of a beloved person — the distinction between a wonderful gift and a cross is not set aside. This radical difference belongs essentially to the meaning and function of God's Providence. Therefore, gratitude is the response to all the positive gifts and submissive, loving acceptance is the response to the crosses.

We should not ignore the different "faces" of God's Providence, as it were; we should not pass over them and respond to them as though there were no fundamental difference between them. Let us not forget that in the positive gifts and especially in grace, there shines forth a distant reflection of eternity, which points to eternal beatitude and even contains a kind of promise of eternal beatitude. All sufferings and crosses, on the other hand, point to the vale of tears and the transitory condition of earthly pilgrimage. The submissive acceptance of this should purify us and unite us with the suffering Christ.[33] But this is only possible if the crosses are fully suffered, if we do not force a joyful response to them.

---

[33] When we say that sorrows are limited to the *status viae*, this may appear to be a serious neglect of Purgatory and Hell. But we are here discussing sorrows and crosses that are a test of human beings, an opportunity to achieve a final surrender to God, and the abandonment of all inappropriate attachments. The nature of the temporary is inherent in these sorrows and in the preparation for eternal bliss. The same is also true of Purgatory, which is concerned with atonement for sin and with purgation with a view to eternal bliss. The relativity of these sufferings appears clearly in their essential relationship to eternal bliss. As for eternal punishment in Hell, this suffering is certainly neither temporary nor a way to eternal bliss. It is concerned with punishment, the divine response to the fearful disharmony of sin, the final rejection of God, and rebellion against Him. The essence and intent of this suffering are radically different from all the crosses God imposes on us on earth, which we know are a result of His merciful love. Hell's sufferings are a result of God's justice. In the *Divine Comedy*, Dante adds love to justice in the words appearing as an inscription above the gate of Hell in Canto 3 of the *Inferno: Giustizia mosse il mio alto fattore; / fecemi la divina potestate, / la somma sapienza e 'l primo amore.* (Justice moved my lofty creator; / I was made by the divine power, / by the highest wisdom and the primal love.)

The Art of Living

The distinction between gratitude and submissive acceptance also becomes clear in its profundity when we bear in mind that we are permitted to ask God in the same way for His positive gifts and for the averting of sufferings and crosses, whereas we are only permitted to ask to suffer crosses if a special vocation is present. We thereby touch upon another great danger that threatens the religious life: eccentricity and artificiality. Things that are genuine, impressive, and beautiful when a special vocation is present are, without such a vocation, eccentric and artificial.

But transformation in Christ, to which all are called, includes the fact that we are permitted to ask for gifts and graces as well as for the averting of crosses and sufferings. "Save us from disease, hunger and war, O Lord," prays the holy Church in the Litany of All Saints. Jesus' prayer in Gethsemane is the model for transformation in Christ. First our Lord prays for the averting of the cup of the most profound sorrow; then, in the final words ("Nevertheless not my will, but thine, be done"[34]) He shows His ultimate submission to the will of God, His unconditional resignation.

> Yet, only in light of the ultimate abandonment to God embodied in the final words, "Not my will, but Thine be done," does the foregoing petition assume its full impact; and only through the earlier petition do the final words assume their full, authentic reality and their glorious truth.[35]

For this reason, gratitude as the response to all positive gifts must be grounded in the same attitude as the submissive acceptance of all sufferings and crosses: in readiness for the unconditional acceptance of that which God imposes on us. But this

[34] Luke 22:42.

[35] Dietrich von Hildebrand, *The Sacred Heart: An Analysis of Human and Divine Affectivity* (Baltimore: Helicon, 1965), 154-155.

ultimate word, "Thy will be done," still does not erase the distinctions between gratitude, loving acceptance, and full suffering of the cross, even when it leads to the cry of dereliction: "My God, my God, why hast thou forsaken me?"[36]

It is of the greatest significance for the relationship of man to God, as He intended it, that the positive gifts not be forgotten among the trials and sorrows. Gratitude and thanksgiving for all positive gifts must live on together with the humble, loving acceptance of the crosses in the light of the Passion of Christ.

There are special cases when acts of Providence that are painful later result in a good for us. This change of aspect, in which something which is in itself an evil later proves to bring about felicitous results, is a special mystery in the course of our lives. Most people can list numerous examples of events in which consequences changed the character of the objective good or evil.

Good consequences do not transform evil into good

But we first must add that such a change does not mean that the positive consequences of the imposed trial revoke its status as an objective evil for us. The change in aspect proceeds from consequences — and they are not necessarily connected to the evil. These consequences are not something that necessarily flows from the trial as such, but are rather a part of that mysterious chain of causality that permeates our life. Therefore, it is fully appropriate when our immediate response to the trial is not gratitude, but a submissive, humble "Thy will be done" accompanied by the belief that this trial will turn out to be a special manifestation of God's love. If, later, happy consequences come to pass, we can give thanks for the trials.

[36] Matt. 27:46.

Gratitude could never be appropriate for some crosses

Secondly, it must be emphasized that there are trials, sufferings, and crosses that are so terrible, so profound, that they can never because of their consequences appear to be positive — for example, the death of the most beloved person, a spouse loved more than anyone else. Even if later, after this trial, a very happy new marriage becomes possible, it would certainly be terrible to give thanks for the death of the first beloved spouse. Even ignoring the fact that such an evil affects not only the survivor but the most beloved, the cross is so severe that it can never be viewed in the light of happy consequences.[37]

We should have particular gratitude for the *magnalia Dei*

We cannot conclude the investigation of gratitude toward God in the life of the person transformed in Christ without referring to gratitude for the *magnalia Dei* in the special sense of this expression (that is, for the supernatural gifts of God).

We have already spoken of the primary gift of our natural life, of our existence as a human person. Now we must consider the still more sublime gift of sanctifying grace, of being born again in Christ. In gratitude for these *magnalia Dei*, a prayer of the Tridentine Mass says "God, Thou hast wonderfully established the dignity of human nature and still more wonderfully renewed it." These special divine gifts extend from the revelation of the Old

[37] There are many cases in which crosses that are not so clear-cut as the ones described above later prove to be manifestations of God's love, so that the concerned person may even thank God for them. But this kind of gratitude is quite different from the normal joyful gratitude that is a reply to God's beneficial gifts. It is a reply to God's love that is manifest in His divine Providence, not a reply to the cross or trial as such.

Testament to God's self-revelation in the sacred humanity of Jesus Christ; they include the most central mystery of the Incarnation and the redemption of mankind through Christ's death on the Cross. They also include the gift of the implanting of supernatural life into the soul of the person in the sacrament of Baptism, the Eucharist, and all the sacraments. Through these gifts, we arrive at an entirely new kind of gratitude. Gratitude for the *magnalia Dei* stands at the central point of the official thanksgiving of the holy Church. This finds its special expression in the prefaces of the holy Mass.

But gratitude for the *magnalia Dei* should also have first place in the private life of the person transformed in Christ. Thanksgiving for them should permeate his life. Let us not forget that through the *magnalia Dei* even our natural life and all natural goods gain a new meaning, a new glory, and that a transfigured light falls upon them. Through the establishment of all things in Christ,[38] entirely new possibilities come into being for man: not only all-pervading hope, but also the capacity to love in God and in Jesus, which first gives to the love of created beings the chance to realize its deepest genius, its ultimate *intentio unionis* (intention of union) and *intentio benevolentiae* (intention of benevolence). The words of Jesus in the book of Revelation, "Behold, I make all things new,"[39] hold true for all of human life and for the transfiguration of all high natural goods in Christ.

Gratitude to other persons is essential for holiness

Having pointed out the fundamental significance of gratitude toward God and shown that the person transformed in Christ is

[38] Eph. 1:10.
[39] Rev. 21:5.

one who gives thanks, that his heart must be filled by this primary attitude of gratitude toward God and toward the God-man Jesus Christ, we now turn to the question: what is the role of gratitude in a person transformed in Christ toward those people to whom he owes much in many ways?

The person transformed in Christ must also be grateful toward all those to whom he is indebted. He must have no hesitation about explicitly giving thanks for all kinds of benefits. Gratitude toward men in whom there is an objective reason for gratitude is the bearer of a high moral value. It is a consequence of humility, goodness, and true freedom. This virtue is indispensable for the one transformed in Christ, not only because it is the bearer of a high moral value, but also because it is a necessary component of holiness.

A man who is reluctant to be grateful to others, feeling this to be a burdensome dependence, is still a slave of his pride. Whoever is so imprisoned in himself that he takes all favors for granted lacks true awareness and freedom. His disregard of the obligation to give thanks, his insensitivity to the generosity contained in every gift, also shows that he himself has not yet fully entered into the kingdom of goodness.

Gratitude differs according to the relationship of persons

In order to see all of this clearly we must begin by distinguishing entirely different cases. The first concerns gratitude toward a person with whom no special friendship or mutual love unites me, who nevertheless renders a great, tangible benefit to me, whether it be moral support in a difficult inner sorrow or a defense against unjust accusations and defamations.

It is interesting that within this first case the nature of the benefit is also a factor. It is more difficult to be grateful for certain benefits than for others. Someone may feel gratitude for financial help, but have difficulty acknowledging his indebtedness toward others in a spiritual respect or even feeling genuine gratitude for that reason.

The second case raises the question: how deep is our gratitude for gifts of all kinds within the framework of a reciprocal, deep relationship, whatever the category of this love? How deeply do each of the partners value the help and gifts of the other?

At this point gratitude demands a different kind of awareness because the danger of taking things for granted, of a failure to realize one's obligation to give explicit thanks for a gift, is greater. This is particularly so in marriage, but it also applies when friends, brothers and sisters, or children and parents, live together. In short, to be alert to the obligation to express gratitude becomes more difficult whenever people are united by a deep mutual love and also live together sharing everyday life. Furthermore, our resistance to gratitude and to explicit thanksgiving will vary according to the nature of the benefits bestowed.

Finally, the third case involves relationships in which, in the love of the one, gratitude toward the other is a constitutive element. Such relationships are shaped from the very beginning by the grateful upward glance of the grateful person toward the one to whom he is grateful.

Pride may yield resentment rather than gratitude for gifts

Let us now consider the first case, namely: gratitude toward someone with whom we are not linked by an intimate relationship. An example would be receiving financial assistance or help in a dangerous situation or being defended by someone when we are wrongly accused. If someone refuses to acknowledge such a debt of gratitude and finds it difficult to admit this dependence on another, it indicates an alarming degree of pride. If the generosity of the other does not move and gratify the recipient, then his heart is still hardened and imprisoned in pride.

Pride struggles against the bond that is implied in being indebted to another. The notion that one owes something to another, that one might even have to reciprocate if a similar situation would arise for the other, is felt as a restriction of freedom and independence. The situation of the helper in relation to the one he helps clearly includes a form of ascendency on the part of the helper. It is deeply characteristic of pride that the beauty of the helper's generosity is ignored and only a resentment against his formal superiority is felt.

There are still other distinctions to be made. For example, the worst kind of ingratitude exists when the very generosity of the helper incurs resentment. The help is indeed accepted, because there is no other way out of the difficult situation, but one already takes offense at the superiority implied by the moral value of the benefactor. This is followed by the desire to misinterpret, to repress, or to deny the generosity involved.

In another case, the recipient does not feel resentment against the benefactor's generosity, but finds it unbearable to be indebted to him. As long as the man's generosity manifests itself in kindness toward others, he will take no offense at it and will perhaps even extol it. But as soon as he is confronted by the superior position of the benefactor, his pride will put up his defenses.

A third, less proud, person would "swallow" this formal superiority if it did not put him under obligation to the other. This person is not so ungrateful that he cannot grasp the debt of gratitude arising from his acceptance of the benefit. He feels the reality of this bond. But in his perverted urge for freedom, in his need for unconditional independence, his primary perception of the debt of gratitude is that it is oppressive. A Hindu saying clearly expresses this form of resistance against gratitude: "Why are you persecuting me? I have never done you a favor."[40]

Fourthly, a person can avoid the consequences of the debt of gratitude out of laziness. He imagines that in a corresponding case he would have to assist the benefactor who, should the need arise, could justifiably demand something from him. The bond is not so much felt to be humiliating or confining but, above all, to be burdensome.

This type will prefer to get out of difficulty any other way, without help from anyone. He is not as amoral as the one enslaved by pride. He even understands that a debt of gratitude has arisen from the favor and does not try to repress it. But it depresses him to have to accept the help of a benefactor because he wants to evade the onerous and troublesome bond.

Humility delights both in gifts and the giver

In contrast to all these who are caught up in pride, who make an idol of independence, or who are mired in egotistical laziness, the person transformed in Christ gratefully accepts the help of the benefactor. He sees the beauty of the other person's kindness and rejoices over it, finding that this generosity is in itself, independently of his being freed from his difficulty, a source of joy and

---

[40] We could also cite other classical references: Tacitus, *Annals*, 4.18: "*Nam beneficia eo usque laeta sunt, dum videntur exsolvi posse: ubi multum antevenere, pro gratia odium redditur.*" ("Benefits are agreeable as long as we hope to be able to repay them. If they greatly exceed this point, gratitude is changed into hate.") See also Seneca, *Epistulae morales*, 81.32: "*Nam quia putat turpe non reddere, non vult esse cui, reddat. . . . Nullum est odium perniciosius quam a beneficii violati pudore.*" ("Since he thinks it shameful not to return a favor, he would not like to have to deal with someone to whom he ought to return a favor. . . . There is no more dangerous hate than that of a man who is offended because of a benefit that puts him to shame.")

happiness. He does not perceive being in someone's debt to be a burden. Quite the contrary, the formal superiority of the other is a joy to him, and he considers his life to be enriched by the bond of gratitude. He experiences a profound happiness and a wonderful freedom in being grateful and in the bond that comes into being through the goodness of the other.

The person transformed in Christ would rather receive a beneficial good through the goodness of another than assert his claim to possess it. As long as he receives something which it is his right to demand, the wonderful element of generosity and kindness by the benefactor is lacking. The receiving of a pure gift, which we have no right to demand, is similar to the previously mentioned gifts of God. For we can never assert a right before God; everything that we receive from Him is pure gift.

But even the person transformed in Christ has a justifiable aversion to falling into the bond of an obligation of gratitude toward another, if the "benefactor" is only helping him in order to bring him under his control. Some people use favors to make others dependent on them; then the element of goodness is completely absent. The favor is only rendered in order to force the other to comply with the wishes of the "benefactor" through the dependency of gratitude. If the "benefactor" is of such a kind, then we are obliged to avoid this dependency. If this is impossible, then we may accept the favor, but we must not concede any sort of power to him that would induce us to do something against our conscience. We must never pay the price of surrendering a right bestowed by God. We cannot really be grateful to such a "benefactor" because, instead of kindness, there is only guile and deceit. We cannot accept any sort of obligation, even if we have to accept the benefit, because the latter is the fruit of an evil disposition, not of kindness, and thus does not bear an objectively true obligation for gratitude.

A characteristic of the moral-religious stance of a person is whether he understands that he is indebted to another, and whether he rejoices at the debt. It is a sign of spiritual wakefulness — so crucial in religious life — that he understands and sees the beauty of the benevolence of the other as a gift, and accepts the demand for gratitude growing out of the favor. At the moment when he no longer takes the charitable act for granted and consciously grasps the goodness inherent in it, he takes an important step in his moral-religious development.

In gratitude there is both a submission *sui generis* (of one's own kind) and a specific magnanimity. Aversion to this submission, the grudging of giving thanks is, to a degree, analogous to avarice.

Love relies on the benevolence of the beloved

To return to the case of gifts within the framework of a lasting relationship grounded in mutual friendship or love: we find that in these relationships a still greater wakefulness is required in order to grasp the obligation for gratitude and to feel the urge to give explicit thanks. The fundamental gift of love shown us by the other, on which the entire relationship is founded, is a boon that cannot be compared with the greatest of benefits. This love is another kind of gift. It is not an effusion of compassion as is the case in an act of help shown to a stranger in need. It is not a manifestation of special generosity, not something that establishes an obligation for gratitude or an indebtedness. This love is in one respect far more than a benefit, while, on the other hand, it is more a gift of God than a gift of the other. For this love, no matter what its category, we primarily thank God who has placed it in our beloved's heart, rather than the beloved, if only because this love does not flow from the latter's free will, like a favor for a stranger or like that love which springs from love of neighbor.

This is another example of the unique *coincidentia oppositorum* (coincidence of opposites). Inherent in all kinds of human relationships built upon mutual love is our knowledge of and belief in the benevolent disposition of the other toward us. We do not expect such a disposition from a stranger; but in every mutual love relationship, we count on the other's readiness to assist us if we need it. Indeed, it is an essential part of our loving concern for the other person that we believe in his readiness to help. This is a necessary element in the love for our partner, and we are hurt and pained when our friend, our sister, our child does not rely on it.

Gratitude is due for the beloved and for his benevolence

How is such a matter-of-course reliance upon the readiness of the beloved to help united with explicit gratitude for every assistance rendered? The paradox between our expectation of benevolent acts as a matter of course and our gratitude for them, which precisely excludes taking them for granted, only appears to be contradictory. We have seen that in all these relationships gratitude primarily refers to the loving disposition of the other toward me. I am grateful that someone is my friend and that I am permitted to be his friend. I am grateful to him for his love, just as I am grateful to my parents, my brother, and my sister for loving me.

Therefore, I am already grateful that I am permitted to expect help in time of need, that I may count on their readiness to help, in contrast to what I may expect from strangers. Genuine gratitude for every assistance, every benefit, flows organically from the benefits received that confirm this wonderful state of reliance on the beloved.

However, taking the act of kindness for granted in no way involves failing to honor our obligation to be grateful for a favor received. It is also not an assertion of a right to the act of kindness.

There is obviously a radical difference between the person who exclaims "What is so special about that after all? True, he helped me, but that is his duty!" and the one who says: "I never doubted that he would help me — he is so good and he loves me." Counting on this assistance as a matter of course is counting on him without hesitation because we have complete faith in him. It is the opposite of the colorless matter-of-factness appropriate for unimportant things. Reliance on the readiness of the other to help includes a value-response to his person and to his love for us. It is the opposite of a neutral calculation; it is a special indication of how highly we value this relationship.

The gift of love calls for profound gratitude

Therefore, such love produces a differently constituted but still deeper obligation. We are still much more profoundly indebted to the beloved, although in another sense. For example, we cannot thank someone who has saved us from a mortal danger enough, and we also cannot reciprocate equally unless God places us in the extraordinary situation in which we can repay like with like. This beneficent act, so clearly defined as such, creates a typical debt of gratitude but one that is entirely different from the obligation arising from personal love. Nevertheless, we should also feel profound gratitude for the unique gift of love. It is a special touchstone for the moral-religious state of man whether he responds with gratitude to the love and fidelity shown toward him. Certainly, he loves the other in the same way. He tenders the same extraordinary surrender of his heart to the other. Of course, we are speaking of a mutual love, whether it be a friendship, love for brothers and sisters, or spousal love. Although we give our heart to the other in the same way that he gives his to us, nevertheless, as a response to his love, a deep form of gratitude should fill our heart.

On the one hand, in an existing mutual relationship of love, there is a kind of right to the love of the other within my surrender to him. The fact that I myself have the same inner attitude toward him and that the attitude is grounded, indeed required, by the nature of the relationship, makes it plain that I have a claim to his love. I expect it; I build upon it; it becomes a foundation of my life. It is the meaningful response to my love. On the other hand, each of the two lovers should regard the love of the other as a gift for which he can never sufficiently give thanks.

In the ideal case, both feel this gratitude, and each knows of the unique form of gratitude in the soul of the other because of the love with which they embrace each other. But this mutual gratitude then leads to the predominant joint gratitude toward God for the reciprocal love, for the mutual relationship, which is His gift.

We perceive the love bestowed on us by the other as a wonderful gift, an acceptance and understanding, a profound comprehension of our true self. We feel that the other has understood our true being and is not wrapped in illusions. At the same time, we feel that we do not deserve this love, that it is an unmerited gift. As is so often the case in the realm of the person transformed in Christ, we again run into a paradox, a coincidence of opposites.

The humble, good, and spiritually free person will feel this special, profound gratitude for the love of the other and know that the demand of this love is the requital of this love. Such a person is aware that no sort of benefit would ever suffice as a response to this call except his similar love, that is, the return of the love of the other.

Charity must permeate love for the beloved

What is the God-willed response for the countless individual gifts rendered by one to the other out of this love? The extent to which our love reveals itself and the way in which our good will takes effect in countless gifts, in loving concern for the other, in our considerateness, in our awareness of his needs and of the degree of his receptivity — all these considerations are extremely revealing of the moral-religious life of a person.

Will the one who loves restrain himself from demanding too much from the other? There is the danger, out of a loving desire to give to the other special joys — to reveal something beautiful to him, to show him a magnificent landscape or piece of architecture — of demanding more than the beloved, according to his physical or spiritual strength, can take in at this moment. The alert, awakened lover will avoid this.

All of this — not only special assistance, gifts, and considerations, but also the desire to bestow beneficial goods on the beloved, from the truly important to the most insignificant attention to his convenience (such as food and the like) — is an indication of the extent to which this love for the other is permeated by *caritas* (charity).[41]

As was stated before, the extent to which love for another manifests itself in these proofs of his good will is very characteristic of a person. This permeation of love by *caritas* is expressed not only in the readiness to accept any sacrifice in order to render a benefit to the beloved, but also in the renunciation of this rendering because the other at the moment needs rest.

Habit and indifference threaten gratitude for love

It is of special significance for our particular problem to understand that one should also be grateful for all these individual

[41] Cf. Dietrich von Hildebrand, *Das Wesen der Liebe*, Ch. 11 (Regensburg: Habbel, 1971), 313-363.

benevolent acts. As already mentioned, it is much more difficult to appreciate the many gifts and assistances of the lover than the extraordinary gifts or benefits on the part of strangers. One is much more inclined to overlook the former.

First of all, one becomes used to them and takes them for granted out of habit. Habit is the one great danger in our moral-religious life: the danger of becoming deadened, of no longer appreciating a gift after a length of time.[42] How dearly we value something that we have not possessed for a long time or that we ardently desired before it was obtained!

Secondly, there is the danger of taking all these benefits for granted and of feeling no obligation for special gratitude because of the attitude which says: "Of course, he loves me, he is so devoted to me; therefore, it is a matter of course that he wants to do me every kind of favor."

Since the love of the other is no longer understood as an extraordinary gift and has, as it were, been fitted into the ordinary components of one's own life, much is expected from this person as a matter of course. In such cases, one may say: "Surely, that is nothing special, as it would be from a stranger; it's the obvious consequence of his love. It gives him joy. I can't be particularly grateful for that." Soon all benevolent actions are seen in this light and thus one feels no obligation for gratitude. Indeed, these proofs of love are eventually overlooked and are no longer even experienced as such.

---

[42] Kierkegaard has a most appropriate comment on this point: "Let the thunder of a hundred cannon remind you three times daily to resist the force of habit . . . but be careful that this also does not become a habit! For you can become accustomed to hearing the thunder of a hundred cannon so that you can sit at table and hear the most trivial, insignificant things far more clearly than the thunder of the hundred cannon — which you have become accustomed to hearing." Soren Kierkegaard, *Works of Love*, trans. Howard and Edna Hong (New York: Harper Torchbooks, 1962), 51.

Gratitude

Gratitude in love presupposes more than other forms

Such ingratitude arises, then, for reasons other than those discussed above. It is motivated neither by pride and resentment against the moral value of the benefactor (which in itself already blocks the value-response to the beauty of his generosity) nor by that pride which abhors being indebted to another, nor by the resistance against the superiority conceded to the other. Neither is it caused by the perverted craving for freedom that denies the obligation of gratitude toward another, nor even by the aversion, resulting from laziness or egotism, to having one's peace disturbed in the future through this dependency.

No, ingratitude for the individual proofs of the love of my friend, my brother, father or mother, or even of my spouse, is first grounded in the universal danger of a developing indifference. It is especially a lack of wakefulness that leads to taking for granted and even overlooking these proofs of generosity and love. It is, furthermore, a lack of love on our part — not only a general lack of wakefulness, but also a "falling asleep" of our love. Since we are no longer awake in our love, the whole image of the other person no longer stands before us so radiantly, and we no longer fully appreciate the gift of his love.

In this form of taking for granted all the beautiful and precious demonstrations of love toward us there also lies a hardening of heart, an offense against the fundamental virtue of goodness. We no longer appreciate the beauty of our partner's loving kindness in all his individual caring acts. We take them for granted, almost as if we had a right to them. This comes out clearly when a person who has grown callous to the loving acts of his partner yet fully appreciates the benefits received from strangers.

We see therefore that full gratitude in a deep, mutual union of hearts presupposes more than does gratitude for the charitable acts of strangers. The former requires a higher moral-religious attitude, a greater wakefulness and goodness, a heart that is more deeply softened. This condition of the heart is only possible in a life *in conspectu Dei* (in the sight of God), which is illuminated by the *lumen Christi* (light of Christ).

Gratitude to others is part of our spiritual transformation

It seems apparent that gratitude toward persons belongs to our transformation in Christ. To be sure, gratitude for the kindnesses of strangers, which can be undercut by pride, is also possible as a natural virtue. But holiness excludes all ingratitude, just as it excludes every other morally negative behavior. Like all natural virtues transformed through Christ, supernatural gratitude receives a completely new radiance and character compared with purely natural gratitude.

Full gratitude in deeper human relationships is only possible in and through Christ. It presupposes a heart formed and softened by gratitude toward God. It is a fruit of transformation in Christ.

How great, how inexhaustible are the goods for which we can be indebted to other men! What truths, what values they can reveal to us! Obviously, we owe special thanks for great gifts that we receive from a friend, from a beloved spouse, and from our parents. The higher the objective good we owe, the more a response of gratitude is morally demanded. Furthermore, more gratitude is due for an act of decisive moral assistance or for profound intellectual encouragement than for an act that saved our life. We should also be grateful for all that we receive through the works and books of those we do not know personally, who may have lived long before us. How much we owe to Plato, St. Augustine, Shakespeare, Cervantes, Bach, and Beethoven! How glorious are Kierkegaard's words about Mozart and everything that he owes to him!⁴³ All the goods that we receive from great figures and geniuses belong in a separate chapter. On a much higher level, the gifts that the saints have given and imparted to the people of their society (and even more to their disciples) are also part of this category.

This brings us to the third type of gratitude, namely, to relationships in which the grateful upward glance of one person to another is an element constitutive of the relationship. To be sure, every relationship has within it a mutual receptivity; there is no relationship in which the person primarily receiving and looking up to the giver does not also bestow something on the latter. To be met with trusting acceptance is already an incomprehensible gift. What a gift is the blossoming of the soul of a beloved person, the bearing fruit of all that the giver, by God's grace, can disclose and impart to him! Truly, this giving, in which what is bestowed is fully received and bears glorious fruits, is at the same time the receiving of a gift.

In addition, there is all that which the receiver gives from his own personality, from the beauty of his unique individuality and, above all, from his love.

These relationships, in which one person looks up to the other, are, in fact, fully mutual, with a full convergence and, above all, a mutual love — although there is a difference in the direction of the affections of the two partners. This difference of direction does not hinder the full synergy and harmony of the mutual love; rather it is complementary. In the person looking up, gratitude is an essential component of his love. He must and ought to be conscious of all that he owes to the donor.

43 Sören Kierkegaard, "The Immediate Stages of the Erotic or the Musical Erotic." In *Either/Or*, Part 1, trans. Howard V. Hong and Edna H. Hong (Princeton: Princeton University Press, 1987).

Of course, a person who is hindered by pride is not capable of such an upward glance. Those who have not been transformed in Christ may in the beginning of the relationship be capable of such an upward glance. However, with the passage of time, a resistance against this respectful upward glance and grateful receiving — or even a rivalry — may develop. Whoever does not have true humility can fall into a certain rebellion and thereby lose true gratitude.

Through gratitude man grows spiritually richer

Man is a receptive being. He has not only received all gifts from God (from his very existence to his free will and his capacity to know and to love); he also receives in a still newer sense all that he can know, all which God reveals to him and men can give to him.

We have often said that a person is as rich as his grasp of values is comprehensive. But we want to stress that it is not only receiving, but also giving that enriches us. In every full value-response we become richer, although our whole attitude is one of giving. This mysterious law finds its supreme expression in the words of Christ: "He who finds his life will lose it, and he who loses his life for my sake will find it."[44] This is also the primary mystery of love: the more someone loves, the more he abandons himself, the richer and deeper he becomes, the more he lives his full personal being.

The same holds true for gratitude, which is a full self-abandonment, a self-donation which in a certain manner constitutes the antithesis to receiving. In it the person becomes richer, in it he grows. "And his riches indeed increase with every time he prays and gives thanks," says Kierkegaard; and shortly before, "How poor

----

[44]Matt. 10:39.

not to be able to pray; how poor not to be able to give thanks; how poor to have to receive everything with ingratitude!"[45]

How right Kierkegaard is, when he emphasizes that it is decisive for man to stand in the right place in the cosmos. Man does this when he gives thanks. Within gratitude lives truth, freedom, humility, goodness, and generosity.

Even in its natural form, gratitude constitutes an essential part of natural morality. But in its transfigured Christian form, in the soul of a person transformed in Christ, it is one of the central virtues and one of the pillars in the relationship of man to God.

Even in its natural form, gratitude leads into the realm of goodness. As long as the person's heart actually overflows with gratitude, there is no room in his soul for evil attitudes like envy, vengefulness, or hatred. But for the person transformed in Christ, this holds true in an entirely new manner in his gratitude toward God and in his gratitude toward man. In true gratitude, the soul shines forth in unparalleled beauty. Like loving, praising, and exalting, giving thanks, belongs to that "which will be in the end without end."[46]

[45] Sören Kierkegaard, *Christian Discourses*, trans. Walter Lowrie (Princeton: Princeton University Press, 1971), 20.

[46] St. Augustine, *The City of God*, Bk. 22, Ch. 30.